)n

The Association for Experiential Education
2885 Aurora Avenue #28/Boulder, CO 80303-2252
(303)440-8844(phone)/(303)440-9581(fax)

KENDALL/HUNT PUBLISHING COMPANY
4050 Westmark Drive   Dubuque, Iowa 52002

This book is printed on recycled paper.

This edition has been printed directly from camera-ready copy.

Copyright © 1990, 1994 by Jasper S. Hunt, Jr.

ISBN 0-8403-9038-6

Printed in the United States of America

10   9   8   7   6

To the Memory of Brad Shaver

Preface to the Second Edition

Since the first edition of this book appeared in 1986 I have benefited a great deal from the feedback I have received. Generally, people have been satisfied with the book. There have been some suggestions made for changes in the book that I have included in the second edition. Many readers wanted the "Ethical Methodology" chapter included in the first chapter rather than saving it until the end. That has been done. There have been specific sentences and paragraphs that I have changed in response to criticism. In many places I have rewritten whole paragraphs in order to eliminate confusion.

Three new chapters have been written for this edition. They are, "Students' Rights," "Social Implications," and "Paternalism." I have had several people comment that this book does not present specific moral stands that I hold personally on the various issues. Some have wanted me to include my own stances on various issues. I have deliberately not included personal stands either in the first edition or in this one. This is because I write primarily as a philosopher here. People who know me know that I hold strong personal convictions on all the issues I have written about. However, when writing as a philosopher, I am forced to present arguments and counter arguments around the various ethical issues. I leave it to the reader to take personal stances, hopefully better informed about the various complexities of the ethical issues involved.

Acknowledgments

I owe thanks to many people who helped make the second edition a possibility. First, I should thank my students who have read the book and who have argued with me about various issues. Their challenges to my thinking have been of immense value.

Dean John Miles of Huxley College of Environmental Studies, Western Washington University, made it possible for me to have the entire original manuscript rekeyed to my computer. His secretary, Ms. Linda Lunow, did the typing and was a pleasure to work with.

I have had some superb proof readers and critics of the manuscript. Special thanks go to Professor Ned Hettinger (Philosophy Department, College of Charleston), Dr. Mitch Sakofs (Outward Bound, USA), Professor Bert Horwood (Faculty of Education, Queens University), Ms. Karen Warren (Hampshire College), and Dr. John Huie, Mr. Don Obert, and Mr. John Flood (all of North Carolina Outward Bound School). These readers have helped clarify my thinking and my writing and I owe them all a debt of gratitude.

Professor Mike Gass (University of New Hampshire) deserves a special mention. Not only has he been a critic and proofreader, he has also been my Association for Experiential Education board liaison. He has been very helpful and supportive throughout this whole process.

Once again, I cannot thank my department chairperson, Professor Bob VanderWilt, enough for all his professional and personal support. The same goes for my college dean, Dean Duane Orr.

My wife, Deen, and sons, Stewart and Pete, have, as usual, always been there providing support and encouragement. Special thanks go to them.

The cover illustration is by David Gross. The book design and production was done by Public Image Design in Boulder, Colorado.

Table of Contents

Introduction

The goal of this book is to encourage experiential education practitioners to reflect carefully on the ethical issues inherent to their profession. Most of the human service professions have spent considerable amounts of time and energy explaining the ethical issues faced by their practitioners. Much has been written about ethics in the fields of medicine, law, psychology, education, social work, and counseling, to name just a few. It is quite appropriate that practitioners in the field of experiential education indulge in a bit of ethical navel gazing in order that we may better serve our students, our organizations, the wider community, and ourselves.

I am not so arrogant or naive to think that ethical reflection has not taken place by experiential education practitioners prior to the publication of this book. My own experience is that experiential educators tend to be among the most ethically concerned people I have ever met. Ad hoc organizational groups have dealt seriously with ethical issues. Instructors in the field make ethical judgments every hour of every day. The ethical dimension permeates the very nature of what we all do with students. I do not claim to have somehow discovered the ethical aspects of experiential education.

However, having made that disclaimer, I do think that there has not been much done in the way of systematic analysis in writing of the ethical dimension as such. I emphasize the words "in writing" because it is in writing about things that we best make our ideas accessible to others. Writing about ethics allows one to present an idea that can be agreed with or disagreed with. It is the reaction of agreement or disagreement that I want to accomplish here, for the reaction gets the argument going. As Socrates said long ago, we must follow the argument where it leads. For this book to be worth the reader's time, the publisher's efforts, and my time, the arguments must lead to clearer thinking about ethical issues in experiential education.

I must add here that the goal of clearer thinking is a modest one on my part. I knew for a fact that I would emerge from writing this book more puzzled about certain things than I was when I started out. I did not intend to produce a Betty Crocker Cookbook of ethics that would provide all the answers in a facile manner. For those who see a book about ethics as providing a cookbook source of specific answers to specific problems, this book will be very disappointing.

On the other hand, I did not want to indulge in too much philosophical rumination to the point of being irrelevant to a practitioner in the field. I hope that the various arguments encountered will be useful to those making the hard decisions.

This book was written for practitioners of experiential education, not for professors of ethics. It is germane to mention here that I was a practitioner in the field of experiential education for several years before I ever read anything about ethical theory. In a sense, this book was written for myself, the self that teaches rock climbing, builds ropes courses, conducts seminars, and works with students on a daily basis. My theoretical side was a handmaiden to my practical side throughout this book.

I worried about the best way to begin the content of this book. The standard works in medical ethics, for example, usually start out with a chapter on theoretical ethics followed by chapters on practical applications and case studies. I was hesitant to use this approach for fear of losing my readers with too much abstraction too early. However, I always teach belaying before I teach rock climbing, my rationale being that one cannot safely rock climb without having been taught belaying. Similarly, I cannot discuss ethical issues in experiential education without discussing ethics first. Therefore, the ethical theory chapter precedes the specific ethical issues in experiential education.

The ethical theory chapter includes a methodology for resolving ethical problems. A criticism that I have had of some ethics books is their lack of practical suggestions for practitioners. Therefore, I have written the ethical methodology section to help facilitate direct applications of ethics to concrete situations.

I have included a large number of examples to illustrate the various ethical issues. Readers should know that all of these examples are from real life situations with students. All names used in the examples are fictitious, but the cases are real.

I am keenly aware that experiential education is a broad concept. Many of the practical examples I have cited come from the wilderness-based wing of experiential education. I have cited wilderness-based examples to a large extent simply because that is the area where I have had the most practical experience. Just because an example came from a program that is wilderness-based, however, need not preclude its usefulness for other types of experiential education. I am convinced that all of the issues covered in this book apply equally well to all areas of experiential education.

I must make a few comments about writing style. The issue of sexist language is a problem. I refuse to adopt the practice of using the words "they" or "them" when referring to a particular person. I use the words "she" and "he" when referring to individuals. Those two words are changed periodically throughout the book. This reflects my sensitivity to the sexist writing issue, while at the same time respecting the integrity of the English language.

Finally, I know there are major ethical issues in experiential education that I have missed. That's the nature of ethics. Just as the Common Peer Practices book, published by the Association for Experiential Education, needed revision from the moment it was published, so too will this book need instant revision once it has been published.

Ethical Theory: The Nature of Ethics

As a doctoral student in education and philosophy, I had several opportunities to teach introductory ethical theory to undergraduates. Invariably, the following scenario would take place. I would make a statement, or take a stand, on an ethical issue. Some rosy-faced young student would raise his or her hand and announce gleefully, "But, that's just a value judgment" or "But, that's just your values" or "But, who's to say" or "Who are we to judge" or "Who am I to judge." The gleeful tone to the voice inflection stemmed from the assumption of the student that, of course, these utterances would render the stupid instructor silent. Naturally, reasoned the student, judgments of value or judgments about right and wrong had no intellectual worth. My standard reply to this ubiquitous sort of answer would be, "Yes, and I enjoy torturing babies for my own pleasure and, furthermore, you cannot condemn me for my delight in torturing this baby. Right?"

"No! That's not what I mean!" the student would answer, horrified at my example.

"Well," I would say, "You just told me that value judgments have no worth. So, how can you object to my delight in baby torturing?"

"Because, torturing babies is wrong," the angry student would say.

"Ah," I would reply, "But, why is it wrong?"

"Because . . ." the student would begin.

"Now, we are doing ethics." I would answer.

The study of ethics is the study of why one state of affairs is morally better or worse than another state of affairs. Once I begin giving reasons why torturing babies for fun is wrong, then I am doing ethics.

In my discussions with experiential educators over the last few years, I have

Chapter One / Ethical Theory

often been stopped early on in ethical discussions by the problem of nomenclature. I am often asked about the distinction between the words "ethic" and "moral." People often express a need to differentiate between ethics and morals. Are we discussing ethics or morals, I am asked. The distinction between the words "moral" and "ethical" is historical. "Moral" comes from a Latin root and "ethical" comes from a Greek root. For the purposes of this book, I shall use the terms moral and ethical interchangeably. It is important, however, to be clear about the distinction between a problem of fact and a problem of value or ethics. For instance, if I assert the proposition that all school children in the United States receive moral education and the truth or falsity of that proposition is called into question, there exists an empirical means to refute or affirm the truth of the proposition. Simply having a researcher measure whether or not all children receive this sort of instruction will settle the issue. Questions of fact are rendered true or false by means of empirical verification.

On the other hand, I might assert the proposition that all American school children ought to receive moral education. If that proposition is called into question, then I am left with the problem of replying to my questioner why school children ought to receive moral education. Simply taking a research survey will not answer the question of what ought to be. Questions of ethics or values are not settled exclusively by means of empirical inquiry. To attempt to answer the question of what ought to be requires a philosophical response rather than an empirical response.

This is not to suggest that there is no connection between ethical problems and empirical information. On the contrary, empirical information is usually vital to the ethicist. I am reminded here of the spectacle of opponents in the abortion issue putting their respective gynecologists on display. The pro-choicers bring out their physician who says various things about the pro-choice position. Then the pro-lifers bring out their physician who says various things about the pro-life position. The point is that the empirical knowledge of the gynecologists, while relevant to the abortion issue, does not resolve the issue. Empirically, both gynecologists presumably have the same information. Yet, they have very different positions on the abortion issue. The conflict between the two physicians resides in issues of ethics and value, not primarily in empirical disagreements.

The work of the ethicist is to help clarify what the ethical issues are (as distinct from the empirical issues) and then to reach reasonable conclusions about what ought to be.

In the effort to clarify issues and to reach conclusions about what ought to be, a warning must be issued. Probably the single biggest obstacle to ethical discourse lies in the efforts of some to demand a degree of certainty and rigor that ethics cannot deliver. A quote from Aristotle's ethics comes to mind here:

Our discussion will be adequate if it has as much clearness as the subject-matter admits of, for precision is not to be sought for alike in all discussions, any more than in all the products of the crafts.

-and later-

. . . for it is the mark of an educated man to look for precision in each class of things just so far as the nature of the subject admits; it is evidently equally foolish to accept probable reasoning from a mathematician and to demand from a rhetorician scientific proofs. [1]

Aristotle's point is that it is right and proper to expect the mathematician to give definite, unequivocal answers to mathematical problems. The nature of mathematics permits such exactness. However, ethics has a different nature from mathematics. Given the mind-boggling complexity of ethics, it is improper to expect the ethicist to deliver the same exact conclusions that can be expected of the mathematician.

The desire for ethical certitude is pervasive and seductive. If we could only be absolutely certain about everything, then we would be relieved of the burden of careful thought about a complex world. Here, I am contrasting the young student of ethics who, at first, does not believe anything, to the other extreme of the know-it-all types. This extreme is represented by the person who refuses to see another side and who thinks ethics is just like mathematics, with clear and distinct results obtained with absolute certainty. As the philosopher Alfred North Whitehead said, "...the chief error in philosophy is overstatement." [2] I believe that the chief error in ethics is overstatement.

So we are left with a difficult tension. On the one hand, we must be able to make ethical judgments and on the other hand we are confronted by a subject that is elusive by nature. Judgments must be made, yet the criteria and methods by which these judgments are made have never been agreed upon in the history of humankind. However, it is useful in a book like this one to understand some of the dominant forces that have been in contention for the status of chief arbitrator in ethics.

The Sources of Ethics

A fundamental issue in ethical theory that should be confronted by experiential educators is the sources of morality. From what ground does the good come? (I am, of course, assuming here that experiential educators are chiefly concerned with doing good rather than evil.) The answers given to the problem of the sources of morality are varied and diverse. I could spend the rest of this book on just this subject. For the sake of brevity, however, I discuss the issue of the source of morality in terms of four different approaches. These four approaches are:

1) Ethical Subjectivism
2) Ethical Objectivism
3) Consequentialist Theories of Ethics
4) Nonconsequentialist Theories of Ethics

Ethical Subjectivism

The ethical subjectivist reasons that in order for an action to be declared a good action, there must be a person who holds that the action is good. The source of morality for the subjectivist is the individual person. It is useful to recall here the Greek philosopher, Protagoras, who said, "man is the measure of all things alike of the being of things that are and of the not-being of things that are not."[3] There is nothing new about ethical subjectivism; it's been in existence for a long time.

The subjectivist's position can take various forms and is a more complex matter than it appears at first. For instance, when asked why she believes so-and-so is good, the subjectivist might reply that it gives her pleasure, or it is in her self interest, or that she simply intuits it. Thus, three different senses of subjectivism emerge: subjective hedonism, subjective egoism, and subjective intuitionism. Although these three senses of subjectivism have different emphases, what is common to them is that the person bases her judgment of goodness, and therefore, moral worth, upon her own self.

The classic and most striking example of the subjectivist position in ethical thought was the Scottish philosopher, David Hume (1711-1776). He writes:

Take any action allow'd to be vicious: Wilful Murder, for instance. Examine it in all lights, and see if you can find that matter of fact, or real existence, which you call vice. In which-ever way you take it, you find only certain passions, motives, volitions and thoughts. There is no other matter of fact in the case. The vice entirely escapes you, as long as you consider the object. You never can find it, till you turn your reflexion into your own breast, and find a sentiment of disapprobation, which arises in you, towards this action. Here is a matter of fact; but 'tis the object of feeling, not of reason. It lies in yourself, not in the object. [4]

It is important to note here that Hume, and subjectivism in general, takes a positive position on the general problem of ethics. The subjectivist answers the query of whether there is any such thing as right and wrong in an affirmative manner. Granted, this affirmation resides exclusively in the self, but it is still an affirmation. This is opposite of the ethical skeptic who, like my hypothetical student in the opening of this chapter, does not believe anything whatsoever about ethics or ethical judgments.

It is the willingness to take a stand on a given issue that includes the subjectivist in the realm of ethics. The subjectivist can take a stand and give reasons why she takes that stand.

The serious problems associated with the subjectivist's position are probably clear to most readers. One of the most devastating attacks that can be made on the ethical subjectivist is the problem of resolving conflicting subjective positions. As a practical matter for experiential educators, one can only wonder at the impossibility of working with students, each of whom believes that matters of morality are resolved privately. No method for reaching agreements exists, although agreement may be reached. If so, then subjectivism becomes workable and it is fortunate. But, if agreement is not made, then insurmountable problems arise.

The logic of necessary and sufficient conditions is useful in the critique of ethical subjectivism. If "A" is a necessary condition for "B," then it follows that without "A" there can be no "B" at all. A necessary condition sets forth a minimum state of affairs that must be met in order for another state of affairs to follow. For instance, being female is a necessary condition for having a baby. Wearing crampons is a necessary condition for being able to climb the Willis Wall on Mt. Rainier. If you are not female, then you cannot have a baby, and if you forget to pack your crampons, you will not make it up the Willis Wall. However, just because a necessary condition has been met, it does not follow logically that something else must follow. Simply being female does not suffice for having a baby and simply putting crampons on one's feet does not ensure that one will be able to climb Mt. Rainier.

In order for "A" to suffice for the entailment of "B," "A" must be a sufficient condition for "B." If I am a resident of North Carolina, then I automatically am also a resident of the United States. Residing in North Carolina becomes a sufficient condition for residing in the United States. Generally speaking, meeting sufficient conditions is much more complex and demanding than meeting necessary conditions. Just imagine what the sufficient conditions are for having a baby or climbing Mt. Rainier by the Willis Wall route.

The ethical subjectivist maintains that if a person claims that an act is a good act, then that claim is a sufficient condition for the act being good. The necessary condition of a good act is that there must be a person who either approves or disapproves of that act.

Another devastating critique of subjectivism emerges here. What happens if the subjectivist is wrong about what she approves? For instance, suppose a person approves of something at 12:00 and changes her mind at 2:00. If what she approved of at 12:00 was good then, what happened at 2:00? Does having been wrong at 12:00 imply that what she thought was good was in fact wrong? In other words, simply holding something as good at 12:00 was not sufficient for being good. This could go on endlessly. Suppose at 3:00 I disapprove of what I approved of at 2:00 and then at 4:00 and so on. The point is that what the subjectivist holds as a sufficient condition for goodness does not work as sufficient at all.

It should be clear that there are both practical and logical problems with ethical subjectivism. Practically, there is the problem of never reaching agreement about anything and logically there is the problem of never finding conditions that are sufficient for subjectivist judgments to be ethically true.

On a less technical level, many people simply feel dissatisfied in resting their ethical fates in subjective judgements. It seems intuitively false that just because a Nazi subjectively judges that it is morally good to kill babies in gas chambers, that it is, therefore, good. Ethical subjectivism renders the whole goal of ethics as discerning good from evil impossible.

In closing, it is my own experience that ethical subjectivism is very common in our culture. Just as there is nothing new about the subjectivist's position, there is nothing unusual about my experience on the pervasiveness of ethical subjectivism. Whenever ethics is reduced to a matter of merely how a person subjectively feels, then ethical subjectivism is alive and well. I am reminded of a recent conversation with a high school guidance counselor who told me that whenever she leads students in values clarification exercises, she never makes judgments about the values that are held. She was proud of the fact that she never makes judgments, for, of course, all values and ethics are subjective.

Ethical Objectivism

The ethical objectivist maintains that in order for an act to be a good act, it must have been made in accordance with some source of morality that transcends the limitations of a particular person or set of limited circumstances. One of the best ways to become clear about ethical objectivists, is to compare them to mathematicians. A mathematician will argue that the formula 2 + 2 = 4 is true whether or not a particular person believes that it is true. If I maintain that 2 + 2 = 11, then I am simply mistaken in my judgment about this proposition. In short, it is true, objectively, that 2 + 2 = 4, whether or not I believe that it is true. The truths of mathematicians provide an objective point of reference, against which I can test the truth or falsity of my own beliefs.

An ethical objectivist reasons almost like a mathematician. He argues that just because I say that a particular action is morally good, it does not necessarily follow that, in fact, it is morally good. Just as I can be mistaken in my mathematical reasoning, I can be mistaken in my moral judgments, according to the ethical objectivist.

This is not to imply that ethical objectivism and the judgments made by an individual can never be the same. An objectivist and a subjectivist might agree on the goodness or badness of a given moral action. It is not the agreement that is important here. What is vital are the reasons given by the two people about why an action is good or bad. The objectivist will not judge good or bad based upon his own feelings about the act. Rather, he will judge the act based upon the application of some source of ethics outside of himself. The subjectivist, while in essential agreement with the objectivist, will base his judgment upon his own feelings. Thus, they agree on the judgment, but not on the reasons behind the judgment.

There are many possible sources upon which to base an objectivist theory of ethics. In the Western historical tradition, two major examples come to mind immediately as illustrations of objective sources of morality.

Recall my reference to Protagoras in the section on subjectivism where he asserts that man is the measure of all things. Just as the subjectivist position was alive and well in ancient Greece, so, too, was the objectivist position alive and well. One of the most famous sources of objectivist ethics came as a direct response to the Protagorean position that man is the measure of all things. Plato (through the voice of Socrates) offered an alternative basis of ethics. Following the lead of the mathematicians, Plato argued that moral truths are as objective as are mathematical truths. To disagree with the objective truths of morality would be as wrong as to disagree with the truths of mathematics. The source of ethics, argued Plato, lay in The Good. Indeed in the Platonic tradition, The Good was the source not only of ethics, but also of truth and reason:

But at any rate, my dream as it appears to me is that in the region of the known the last thing to be seen and hardly seen is the idea of good, and that when seen it must needs point us to the conclusion that this is indeed the cause for all things, of all that is right and beautiful, giving birth in the visible world to light, and the author of light and itself in the intelligible world being the authentic source of truth and reason, and that anyone who is to act wisely in private or public must have caught sight of this.[5]

Just as there is a distinction between the source of morality for the objectivist and the subjectivist, there is also a distinction between them in how the good is known. For the Protagorean or Humean subjectivist, good is known through one's personal feelings about things. For the Platonic objectivist, the good is known through reason.

A second major source of objectivist ethical theory in the Western tradition is the Judeo-Christian religious tradition. Although there are numerous instances of ethical objectivism at work in this tradition, one event stands out in illustrating this point. I am referring to the giving of the Ten Commandments to the Hebrew people in Exodus 19 and 20 of the Old Testament. Moses, the leader of the Hebrews, states these words after having received the Ten Commandments:

"Do not fear; for God has come to prove you, and that the fear of him may be before your eyes, that you may not sin." [6]

One of the key points of the whole Hebrew ethical and religious tradition is that ethics is not simply a matter of personal, subjective preference. Ethics is a matter of clearly defined sources of morality that are not determined by the vicissitudes of subjective fiat. The bottom line in ethics for most people operating within the Judeo-Christian tradition is that the good action is action taken in accord with the will of God. As the Hebrew writer puts it:

Trust in the Lord with all your heart, and do not rely on your own insight. In all your ways acknowledge him, and he will make straight your paths. Be not wise in your own eyes; fear the Lord, and turn away from evil. It will be healing to your flesh and refreshment to your bones. [7]

The Protagorean or Humean subjectivist knows the good through personal feelings and the Platonic objectivist knows the good through reason. The Judeo-Christian objectivist knows the good through faith. Although Plato and the Hebrew writer are agreed that ethics is objective, they differ on how the good is known. The conflict between faith and reason in this example of ethics touches on one of the key controversies in all of Western culture as well as ethical theory.

The complexity of all this is staggering. Even within the broad scope of ethical objectivism, the competing voices about what the good is in a given action are too numerous to comprehend. Just imagine the variety of objectivist positions that could be taken on the abortion issue.

One issue that always comes up in discussions of ethical theory is the problem of cultural relativism. The cultural relativist argues that good and evil can be judged only in terms of local cultural standards. The problem here is whether cultural relativism is objective or subjective. I have included the cultural relativism issue under the heading of ethical objectivism because I am convinced that the cultural relativist is usually an ethical objectivist.

Cultural relativism is objective when the actions judged as good or bad within that culture are determined by the standards of that culture, not by individual subjective feelings. The cultural strictures on right and wrong serve as an objective source of ethics within that culture.

It is important not to confuse an objective ethical theory with a universal ethical theory. This is a common confusion. It is often thought that ethical objectivism logically implies a universal theory of ethics. By universal, I mean a theory of ethics that applies regardless of the vagaries of different situations, cultures, nations, or contexts. For instance, the truth of the mathematical proposition $2 + 2 = 4$ can be called an objective truth that is also universal. However, ethical truths can be objective and not universal. For instance, a student might join an athletic team that has a stricture against consumption of carbonated beverages. Once the student has joined this team, the moral imperative not to consume carbonated beverages becomes objective for him or her. But, one would hardly declare that the injunction is a universal one. The child's parents, for instance, can hardly be held to this standard of conduct.

In short, objectivist theories of ethics may or may not be universal. However, the converse is not the case. A universal ethical truth is by definition objective.

This is where cultural relativism becomes a problem in ethical theory. Although certain actions may be acceptable in a given culture, it does not follow that these actions are universally acceptable. Before the American Civil War, slavery was believed to be morally acceptable in certain states. This was objectively acceptable. However, it was highly questionable whether it was also universally acceptable. One of the bloodiest wars of American history was fought over precisely this problem of cultural relativism.

If there were severe problems with subjectivist theories of ethics, there are equally severe problems with ethical objectivism. Recall my first criticism of subjectivism concerning the problem of resolving differing claims about the good. The same problem holds true for objective theories. Although all ethical objectivists would agree that morality is not merely subjective, that is about all they would agree on. There are probably nearly as many differing theories of what the objective sources of ethics are, as there are competing subjectivists. Just agreeing that ethical truths are objective does not accomplish very much. Even within a given tradition of ethical objectivism, great conflict can emerge about what these objective truths are. For instance, within the Judeo-Christian tradition, several thousand different and identifiable sects exist, many of which hold violently conflicting moral positions. Yet they all claim to be based upon objective moral foundations.

A corollary issue is the problem of how objective ethical truths are known. What they are and how they are known are very different issues. The differences between the moral objectivist who claims to know the good through reason and the objectivist who claims to know the will of God through faith can be varied.

Another problem of ethical objectivism is in the area of ethical casuistry. Casuistry is the study of the application of general moral truths to specific cases. The problem of casuistry is a thorny one for the ethical objectivist. For instance, take the injunction from the Ten Commandments not to lie or bear false witness. For those operating within the Judeo-Christian tradition, this commandment exists as an objective moral truth. The husband of your neighbor comes to the door of your house one evening. The man has a history of wife beating. He is enraged, drunk, incoherent, and has a knife. He wants you to tell him where his wife is, so he can "teach her a lesson, once and for all." You know that the wife is down the street, strolling in the park. Ought you to lie to the husband about where his wife is, either by denying that you know where she is, or else by steering him in the wrong direction? This sort of case exemplifies the value of ethical casuistry. If the person confronting this case is operating within the objective morality of the Judeo-Christian tradition, and, therefore, believes that "bearing false witness" is objectively wrong, what is he to do? Simply having an objective source of ethics does little to resolve the casuistic problem in this example.

Consequentialist Therories of Ethics

Once the distinction between subjective and objective theories of ethics has been made, another issue arises in ethical theory that is at least as troubling as the conflict between objectivism and subjectivism. Recall that a chief problem for either the subjectivist or objectivist is the problem of determining the good action when conflicts arise between competing positions on a given issue. For the true subjectivist, no means of resolving these conflicts exists. However, the objectivist has at least begun the process of resolving ethical disputes.

One of the most common approaches to the determination of right and wrong is to make judgments in terms of the highest good and its relationship to a given state of affairs. This is called normative ethics. The normative ethicist seeks to know the highest good as the foundation for determining right from wrong. The hope here is that once the highest good is known, then there is at least a point of reference from which to make judgments. In ethical language, the search for the highest good is the search for the summum bonum. As the philosopher John Stuart Mill said about this issue:

There are few circumstances among those which make up the present condition of human knowledge more unlike what might have been expected, or more significant of the backward state in which speculation on the most important subjects still lingers, than the progress which has been made in the decision of the controversy respecting the criterion of right and wrong. From the

dawn of philosophy, the question concerning the summum bonum, or, what is
the same thing, concerning the foundation of morality, has been accounted
the main problem in speculative thought, has occupied the most gifted intel-
lects and divided them into sects and schools, carrying on a vigorous warfare
against one another.[8]

Normative ethics is not only objective; it is also universal. The summum
bonum is not subjectively dependent and it is not relative to anything else. As
Mill points out so very well in the above quote, however, the quest for the
summum bonum is difficult at best.

One of the most famous and widely accepted applications of normative
ethics is through the method of ethical consequentialism. The basic method of
the consequentialist is rather simple. The consequentialist reasons that the
only way to apply the summum bonum to specific cases is in terms of the results
of a given act. If an act has good consequences, in terms of the highest good, then
that act is judged, post facto, a good act. If the act results in bad consequences,
then it was a bad act. The focus in this method is with the results of actions,
rather than with the acts themselves.

Taking a rather far fetched example to illustrate this point, suppose the
summum bonum is neatness and order. I am deciding whether a given
experiential educator is good or bad. In order to judge her, I examine her actions
to see if they result in a neat and orderly educational experience. If neatness and
orderliness result, then I judge her good because she has met the criteria of the
highest good. What she may or may not have done to bring about neatness and
order is not nearly as important as the results that occurred.

The most famous consequentialist theory of ethics operative today is called
Utilitarianism. Fundamentally, the utilitarian argues that actions are good, if
and only if, they bring about the greatest good for the greatest number. The
"greatest good" (summum bonum) for the utilitarian is defined as happiness:

The creed which accepts as the foundation of morals "utility" or the
"greatest happiness principle" holds that actions are right in proportion as they
tend to promote happiness, wrong as they tend to produce the reverse of hap-
piness. By happiness is intended pleasure, and the absence of pain; by
unhappiness, pain, and the privation of pleasure.[9]

Here, Mill links up happiness with the experience of pleasure, unhappiness
with the experience of pain. Thus, the summum bonum of happiness is defined
in terms of pleasure. The good act for the utilitarian, therefore, is the act that
results in a greater degree of happiness measured by the amount of pleasure
produced.

It is critical to note that there are two fundamental pillars of the utilitarian
approach to ethics. As just stated, "happiness" is the first pillar and "for the

Chapter One / Ethical Theory

greatest number" is the second pillar. I emphasize the "for the greatest number" aspect of utilitarianism because it is this two-fold characterization that is used throughout this book. Technically, the "for the greatest number" foundation of utilitarianism is called Universalistic Utilitarianism. This is contrary to Egoistic Utilitarianism, where the happiness of the isolated individual is the focus. Both egoistic and universalistic calculations of pleasure are relevant to ethical issues in experiential education. However, the term utilitarianism has come to mean the "greatest good for the greatest number" formulation. The general good is the focus for the utilitarianism, not just the private good. As the famous utilitarian Henry Sidgwick said:

Here I wish only to point out that, if the duty of aiming at the general happiness is thus taken to include all other duties, as subordinate applications of it, we seem to be again led to the notion of Happiness as an ultimate end categorically prescribed, — only it is now General Happiness and not the private happiness of any individual. And this is the view that I myself take of the Utilitarian principle. [10]

It is probably obvious to most readers that one's private happiness and the happiness of the larger group may often conflict. I shall have more to say throughout this book about the conflict between private and group happiness.

At the close of the section on ethical objectivism, I outlined the case of the drunken wife-beater who wants to know where his wife is so he can teach her a lesson. I presented that case as a troubling one for the objectivist who believes that bearing false witness to the husband is morally wrong. This case is easily resolved by a utilitarian's way of looking at ethics. First, the utilitarian will be more concerned about what his act results in than with the act itself. He will be more concerned with the accomplishment of happiness than with following a specific moral precept. In short, he will look at the consequences of his act to define whether or not the act was a good act. If he thinks that a greater good will result by lying to the husband, then the utilitarian consequentialist will go ahead and lie with a clear conscience. On the other hand, the utilitarian might go ahead and answer the husband truthfully because of the happiness that will accrue to the husband. Which is it? With utilitarianism, a greater happiness takes precedence over a lesser happiness. Most utilitarians would probably argue that it is better to lie to the husband because the happiness experienced by the wife at not being murdered will be much greater than the happiness of the husband at having taught her a lesson.

There is an important distinction within utilitarian ethics that must be made. One train of thought argues that the utilitarian's calculation is only to be used in setting up general standards and institutions of society, and not with particular cases. The question here is, "Does this rule of conduct in general promote the greatest happiness?" If so, then the standard or rule is adopted. This is called Rule Utilitarianism.

The other train of thought is that the utilitarian calculation is used in each moral event that one encounters. The question here is, "Does this particular act satisfy the demands of the summum bonum?" If so, then one acts in accordance with the highest good. This approach is called Act Utilitarianism. The act utilitarian applies the utilitarian calculation specifically and the rule utilitarian applies the calculation to more general rules of conduct.

For instance, the rule utilitarian, when confronted by the example of the wife beater, will be more concerned with the general practice of lying than with the specifics of the given example. On the other hand, the act utilitarian will judge based upon the specific case.

It is important to be clear that not all consequentialist theories of ethics are necessarily utilitarian in nature. A consequentialist theory of ethics is utilitarian when the summum bonum is the greatest happiness for the greatest number. However, it is important to realize that other possibilities exist for the establishment of a summum bonum as definitive of good or bad consequences.

Suppose I am the instructor of a wilderness-based experiential education program for juvenile delinquents. I know that this particular program is paid a set rate of money for each day that a given student stays in the program. I have a particularly troublesome student in my group. He is so disruptive that he is detracting from the quality of the course for the others. I want to kick the student off the course in order to improve the quality for the others. But I know that if I lose this student, my course will fall below the financial break-even mark. Therefore, I keep the student and lower the quality of the course for the other students, but make some much needed money for the overall program. What ultimately determined my action was the need to make money in order to enrich the program. What was the summum bonum in this example? In other words, in what terms did I make my decision? I made the decision, in this example, in terms of financial gain. Therefore, money was my summum bonum. My action, (not kicking the student off the course) resulted in good consequences (financial gain), and therefore was a good action. This is an example of consequentialist ethical thinking from a perspective that is not necessarily utilitarian. The greatest good for the greatest number was replaced by an alternative highest good. This example could be reformulated to make it a utilitarian example if the reasoning behind keeping the student was to benefit an even greater number of students by ensuring greater financial viability for the program. However, as presented initially, the financial survival was pursued for its own sake and not for future students.

There are serious problems with ethical consequentialism in general and with the utilitarian version of consequentialism specifically. The most glaring and obvious problem with consequentialism is the problem of doing bad things in order to achieve good results. This problem is often formulated in terms of "do the ends justify the means?" It is easy to imagine a scenario where genuinely good ends were obtained, consequentially, but where very bad actions were taken to achieve these ends. Let's look at the example of the juvenile delinquency program again. Suppose, in my zeal to achieve the end of financial stability for my program, I keep this student. However, in achieving the end I neglect the other students. I endanger their safety because of this student's recklessness. I burn myself out and become detached from the problems of the other students. In short, a case can be made that although I achieved a good end, I did bad things to achieve this end.

The utilitarian version of consequentialism is also particularly troubling. If the good is defined in terms of the greatest good for the greatest number, then what happens to the interests of the minority? This is a very old conflict and one which has yet to be resolved. A now classic example of the excesses utilitarianism can foster is contained in the following example:

Suppose that an old man of worthless character is in possession of a large fortune, which I can attain by putting him to death, and employ for my own benefit and that of mankind. Why should not I knock the rich villain in the head, and do good with the money, of which he makes no use? The action, by the very terms of the statement, will be a beneficial one. My intentions in committing it, are with a single view to the benefit it will produce. If utility is the criterion, the old miser must die. There is no other way. [11]

There is something repulsive about the ideas expressed in this quote. However, simply finding an idea repulsive is not enough in ethics. Yet the example of the miser illustrates the fundamental flaw inherent in any form of the utilitarian calculation of morality. What is it, exactly, that makes killing the man repulsive? Three ideas emerge as arguments against the utilitarian view presented in the quote. First, to kill the man would be to violate his right to life. Second, to take his money would violate his self-interest in disposing of his money as he pleases. Third, our society has as a fundamental institution, the notion that private property is not to be violated without, as an absolute minimum, some sort of legal due process. Summary execution of an innocent man who has done nothing to forfeit his life, interests, and private property, except be of "worthless character," would be to violate fundamental ethical ideals. Granted these ideals would be violated in the name of good ends. But the nagging question remains - do these ends justify such awful means? The point is that it is difficult for utilitarianism to give reasons why the old man should not be put to death. His private interests, under the scrutiny of the utilitarian calculus, become of secondary importance to the greatest good for the greatest number. Utilitarianism typically cannot account for private and minority interests, except when these interests fit the utilitarian calculation.

Nonconsequentialist Theories of Ethics

The nonconsequentialist approach to ethics is concerned with acts themselves, not with the results of acts. Normatively, the summum bonum for the nonconsequentialist must be the determining factor of the act done. The nonconsequentialist reasons that the post facto approach of the consequentialist must be replaced by an emphasis on the nature of specific acts per se. The fundamental ethical question asked by the nonconsequentialist is not, "What did my action result in?" Rather it is, "What did I do?"

While the question changes, the problem remains, "In what terms are specific acts judged as good or bad?" Acts are judged in terms of their adherence to the standard set by the summum bonum. Once this standard has been determined, it is not to be put aside in order to achieve good ends. The standard becomes operative in the very means used to achieve any given end. In fact, for a strict nonconsequentialist, it would be absurd to grant a judgment of good to an end where the good is not constantly present in the means.

Recall my example of the wilderness-based juvenile delinquency program. As originally set up, the instructor kept the problem student in order to ensure the financial health of the organization. However, an ethical nonconsequentialist might take a very different approach to resolving this issue. The specific action taken would be in accordance with the summum bonum. Suppose the highest good was upholding the civil law during courses. Suppose, also, that part of the problem with this student lay in his violation of various laws while on the course (e.g., he steals other students' cigarettes.) Once confronted with this violation of the law, and therefore the summum bonum, I am compelled to make my ethical judgment. This judgment is not made on results, but on the acts themselves. When I expel the student from the course, am I acting rightly? Yes, if my action itself was a good act. Upholding the law made it a good act.

Two key theoretical sources immediately come to mind as sources of the summum bonum for ethical nonconsequentialists. (Note that there can be a wide variety of sources competing for the highest good, both for ethical consequentialists and nonconsequentialists). Just as the Judeo-Christian religious tradition serves as a foundation for objectivist theories of ethics, it also provides an objective source for ethical nonconsequentialists. (I must assert here that not all of those operating within the Judeo-Christian ethical tradition

Chapter One / Ethical Theory

are nonconsequentialists. Many Jews and Christians are consequentialists. However, I am using a specific interpretation of the Judeo-Christian tradition here to illustrate a possible source of the summum bonum for ethical nonconsequentialism).

It can be argued that the highest good within the Judeo-Christian tradition is the will of God, as discussed earlier in this chapter. Furthermore, it can be argued that the will of God is known by God's commands, revealed through Scripture and the life of the Church. Thus, God's commands illustrate God's will in ethical matters. Therefore, if I am an ethical nonconsequentialist operating within the Judeo-Christian tradition, I act in accordance with God's will revealed through Scripture and the Church. For instance, in Exodus 20 of the Old Testament, the command is given, "You shall not bear false witness against your neighbor."[12] The commandment not to bear false witness means that telling lies is wrong. Notice that the commandment is not amended with an ending that implies telling lies is good when a good result happens. Bearing false witness is, per se, wrong and violates the summum bonum of God's will revealed through Scripture. Acts which are acts of bearing false witness are, in a sense, predetermined to be bad acts because of the standard set by the summum bonum.

The other chief source of thinking in terms of ethical nonconsequentialism is the ethical thought of the German philosopher, Immanuel Kant. There is no doubt that the ethical thinking of Kant is among the most pervasive and influential sources of morality for the Western world. Indeed, Kant's influence ranks in importance just under that of the Judeo-Christian tradition and is of equal status with the thought of J.S. Mill.

There is a threefold progression in Kant's ethical theory for answering the question of, "What makes any act a good act?" This progression results in a summum bonum of very practical applicability to experiential education. The first determination of the good act for Kant is that it must have been made from a sense of duty and not from personal inclination. The concept of duty is so central to Kantian theory of nonconsequentialism that nonconsequentialism has generally been called the deontological theory of ethics. A deontological ethic is simply an ethic of duty. In reference to the importance of duty in ethics, Kant writes:

But beneficence from duty, when no inclination impels it and even when it is opposed by a natural and unconquerable aversion, is practical love, not pathological love; it resides in the will and not in the propensities of feeling, in principles of action and not in tender sympathy; and it alone can be commanded.[13]

It is interesting to note that Kant makes a further ethical thrust in this quote when he suggests that the beneficent act is to be pursued even when it is resisted by "unconquerable aversion." When one acts in accordance with the principle of duty and not from "tender sympathy," then she is acting well, according to the Kantian theory.

The second key element in Kant's threefold ethical progression is the concept of law or ethical principle. One might reasonably ask, "But what is my duty?" To suggest that one act in accordance with duty is well and good. However, duty must be informed by something. That "something" is duty informed by some ethical law or ethical principle. As stated by Kant:

Now as an act from duty wholly excludes the influence of inclination and therewith every object of the will, nothing remains which can determine the will objectively except the law, and nothing subjectively except pure respect for this practical law. This subjective element is the maxim that I ought to follow such a law even if it thwarts all my inclination. [14]

When Kant suggests here that the duty one has must be determined by the law, it is easy and natural to make a critical mistake in interpretation. By "law," Kant does not necessarily mean the civil law. The law or principle Kant is referring to should not be mistaken for civil law. While the law Kant is referring to might coincide with the civil law, it does not come from the same source.

If the law under consideration is not necessarily the civil law, then what is it? The answer to this question leads into the third aspect of the threefold foundation of Kant's nonconsequentialist ethical theory. The law that it is one's duty to follow in all acts is the law contained in the summum bonum. Kant's answer to the problem of the summum bonum, what it is, is what sets him apart from consequentialist theories of ethics.

Since the law that is to be followed is subsumed under the summum bonum, this law must be followed in deciding any moral act. Kant calls this law the categorical imperative. Categorical means that it is to be followed without exception and imperative means that it must be followed for any act to have moral worth:

Finally, there is one imperative which directly commands a certain conduct without making its condition "some" purpose to be reached by it. This imperative is categorical. It concerns not the material of the action and its intended result but the form and the principle from which it results. What is essentially good in it consists in the intention, the result being what it may. This imperative may be called the imperative of morality. [15]

Thus, in order for an act to be a good act, argues Kant, it must have been taken through the normative command of the categorical imperative. Kant says:

There is, therefore, only one categorical imperative. It is: Act only according to that maxim by which you can at the same time will that it should become

Chapter One / Ethical Theory

The summum bonum is the will acting according to the universal moral law, which is the categorical imperative. When I am confronted by a moral problem, I ask myself: "If I could will that this action be universally a law, then is it a good act?" If I could not, then it is a bad act.

Take the example of the drunken wife beater. The categorical imperative demands that I will the lie about telling the husband where his wife is, as a universal law. In short, could I will that lying be universalized as good? If not, then I must choose some action other than that of lying. It is the act of lying that is critical for the Kantian nonconsequentialist and not the results of the act of lying that are so important. If I could not will that all people should go about lying, then I cannot lie in this case.

The Kantian approach to ethics is common and very pervasive in our culture. The categorical imperative, with its universal dictum, can be seen at work in many everyday situations. For example, you approach a person in authority and ask him or her to do some act for you. The person looks at you and says, "But, if I did it for you, I would have to do it for everybody. Since I can't do it for everybody, I can't do it for you." This is the Kantian attitude at work. Now, I am not suggesting that this person is aware that he or she is thinking like Kant. Most people probably have not even heard of the Kantian categorical imperative but they are thinking like a Kantian in their approach to morality.

My main criticism of the utilitarian, consequentialist approach to ethics was that it might justify too much. That is, it might open the ethical floodgates to many bad acts. My main criticism of the ethical nonconsequentialist is that it justifies too little. The idea that acts must be judged on their own merits without regard to consequences, while simplifying complex situations, is rather uncompromising and severe. To use a rather trivial example, imagine being in a marriage and never being able to lie to your spouse. You have planned a surprise birthday party and your spouse asks you what you are doing that night. In order to protect the surprise of the party, you must give a deceptive reply. However, if you are a good Kantian, nonconsequentialist, you cannot lie and you must be honest about what you will be doing that evening. The possible good consequences (the surprise party) are irrelevant to the badness of the act (lying to your wife).

This issue of the rigidity and inflexibility of ethics based on acts can be described in terms of the "ends and means" distinction. For the nonconsequentialist, ends are never the determining factor of the morality of means. That is, the ends do not justify the means. There was an interesting interaction on television recently which illustrates my point. The show was "This Week" with

David Brinkley, produced by ABC news. ABC White House Correspondent Sam Donaldson and ABC News Analyst George Will were arguing about a point of morality. Donaldson asserted that "the ends do not justify the means." George Will snapped back, "Sam, the question is which ends justify which means." For a true nonconsequentialist, Will's retort to Donaldson is nonsense. The differing circumstances implied in the idea of which means and ends have little or no impact upon the morality of any given act.

A Methodology for Resolving Ethical Problems

The ethical analyses applied to the eleven issues in this book (Risk/Benefit, Informed Consent, Deception, Secrecy, Captive Populations, Sexual Issues, Environmental Concerns, Group versus Individual Benefit, Students' Rights, Social Implications, Paternalism) are designed primarily to flush out some of the competing valuational and ethical claims operating in each issue. These eleven issues represent a mere portion of the tip of the iceberg of ethical issues inherent in any form of experiential education. Many other ethical issues are present that I have not touched on in this book.

My goal in the final section of this chapter is to make some suggestions that may be useful to practitioners as they encounter ethical issues in their professional lives. I have stressed the importance and inescapable fact that practitioners must make moral judgments throughout their professional lives. If it is true that moral judgments will be made, then the next problem is how they judgments will be made. What follows are some guidelines that I think may be useful to practitioners. I must add that I recognize the degree to which I am sticking my neck out on the chopping block in this section. Any attempt to present an ethical methodology exposes the person presenting the methodology to violently opposing views on ethics. Few topics raise emotional hackles like topics involving ethics.

My goal is not to present solutions, but only a method for reaching solutions. Anyone who wants to become a lead rock climber must master the art of chock placement and other protective measures. Once this art is mastered, then the climber must deal with the complexities of various rock climbs in different ways. No rock climbing instructor can predict or tell his or her students exactly what challenges they will face on various rock climbs. Chock placement is merely a method of protection. The particular solutions to protection problems on rock can only be made by the leader on the spot.

It is useful to outline some methodological dangers and pitfalls that hinder making good ethical judgments. There are two extremes that, while possibly attractive to some people, stand in the way of a rational approach to ethics.

The first danger is the approach which is purely subjectivistic in nature. This approach eschews any rational resolution to value judgments and relies instead on the force of pure emotion to settle ethical conflicts. Instead of rational arguments, this person simply supplies strong emotional outbursts and hopes that his or her emotions will carry the day. In my view, the purely emotional approach to making ethical judgments ultimately results in the use of violence and force to settle the issue. If my emotions do not sway you, then I will simply back up my emotions with my fist or other violent instruments.

The other extreme that should be avoided when doing ethics is the position of casting an ethical edifice in stone that is not open to any reasonable interpretation. I call this ethical fundamentalism. The ethical fundamentalist, when confronted by a conflict of values, simply looks at the edifice, asks it what to do, and then provides an easy answer. The edifices of the ethical fundamentalist are varied and multitudinous. They may include the word of an exalted leader, the creeds of a given social movement, the dictates of a religious book, a manual of policies and procedures, or some other rigid and uncompromising source of right and wrong. The chief characteristic of the ethical fundamentalist is a refusal to let reasoned argument enter into the making of judgments. Judgments are made only in accordance with a prescribed set of dictates that are exempted from the scrutiny of reasoned analysis. The ethical fundamentalist is the exact opposite of the emotional subjectivist.

The first step in presenting this methodology is the importance of programs and practitioners recognizing some of the ethical issues they will encounter before these programs actally begin. It is my conviction that a person who has thought about ethical matters is better able to handle these matters than is a person who has never thought about them. Making ethical judgments in the heat of the moment without having previously thought about ethics is problematic at best. Therefore, my first positive suggestion for practitioners is that they consciously engage in ethical reflection, apart from the actual work they do professionally. For instance, as staff members in various programs begin planning for their activities with students, it seems vital that they include careful thought about ethical matters as integral parts to the planning process. Too often I have seen discussions of professional ethics relegated to a second class status. This takes the form of allowing a few minutes for ethics after everything else has been completed. My premise is that it is better to be conscious of ethical issues than merely to act unconsciously on them. Experiential educators might take a lesson from medical education. Years ago medical ethics was not even mentioned in medical school, much less taught as an integral part of the curriculum. Presently, most medical schools offer whole courses in medical ethics as an integral part of medical education. The assumption is that physicians who have reflected carefully about ethical issues are better able to deal with situations as they come up, than physicians who have never thought about ethics until they encounter problems in the hospital or clinic.

An excellent way of dealing with ethical issues before the fact is through case studies. Practitioners can be presented with cases containing ethical problems and practice doing an ethical analysis. Judgments can be made and reasons given for making the judgements can be scrutinized. Small group discussions revolving around the case studies can help facilitate instructor awareness of the varied ethical interpretations of a given set of facts.

In order to begin to methodically approach ethical issues in experiential education, it is important that the practitioner gain some sophistication in sorting out what particular ethical issues occur in a given state of affairs. Many times the facts of the case are so closely intertwined with the ethics of the case that it is difficult to sort out the different issues. Earlier in this Chapter I pointed out the spectacle of opponents in the abortion debate trotting out their respective gynecologists, as if the pronouncements of a gynecologist would resolve the ethical issue of abortion. While the knowledge of the physician is very important in making reasoned judgements about abortion, it does not resolve the specific ethical conflicts in the issue. Similarly, in experiential education cases of conflict involving ethics, the facts of the case, while very important, do not necessarily provide enough information to make a judgment.

This points out the need for discovering, as exhaustively as possible, the details of ethically troublesome cases in order to sort out the various valuational and ethical elements present in a given context. For instance, I yell "Fire!" in a crowded movie theatre. I claim that my free speech rights make that yell a moral act. The person who has just been injured in the ensuing panic tells me that he had as much interest in not being hurt as I had in speaking freely. The point is that there are many competing values present in the context of yelling "Fire!" in a movie theatre. In order to make a reasoned judgment about the morality of my act of yelling, it is vital that the facts of the case be ascertained carefully.

It is my assumption that any context involving human beings has within it valuational elements that are possible subjects of ethical analysis. One problem this presents to the ethically concerned practitioner is the problem of selection of important from unimportant ethical issues. A danger in ethical methodology lies in what I call the "ethics of trivia." The "ethics of trivia" is the elevation of basically trivial ethical issues to a level that they do not deserve. In emergency medicine, there is a concept called triage. Triage is the sorting out of different levels of illness and injury in terms of potential for life endangerment. It makes no sense to treat a broken finger while ignoring a cut artery. I think a similar line of reasoning should be applied to ethical issues in experiential education. There should exist a type of ethical triage which will help to avoid the ethics of trivia.

The concept of an ethical triage is extremely controversial. What is ethically important to one person may be unimportant to another. However, the determination of what is important from what is unimportant, while difficult, is vital. My point is simply that there is only so much time to spend discussing ethical matters in our professional lives and it is wise to spend that time on matters of great importance rather than matters of less importance. Issues determined to be trivial might well be left unresolved and left to subjective discretion.

Once the ethical and valuational elements present in a context have been determined, the practitioner is faced with weighing competing claims and evaluating competing arguments. Simply becoming clear about what the ethical problems are does not suffice for making judgments. The problem becomes: in terms of what value do I make my judgments? This leads to an issue of pivotal importance. It is vital for anyone concerned with making ethical judgments that the question of the summum bonum be faced. The individual practitioner and experiential education programs should at the very least ask themselves what constitutes the highest good. I always ask my graduate students to determine what value or values they would die for. Is there any moral grounding in terms of which everything else is secondary? Once that difficult question has been answered, then one has taken a major step toward making reasoned judgments.

Robert E. Lee had to make a judgment between accepting command of the United States Army or accepting command of the Virginian Army at the outbreak of the Civil War. To accept the command of the U. S. Army would mean to try to preserve the Union and to attack the institution of slavery. Lee was on record as detesting slavery. To accept command of the Virginian Army meant to defend slavery. Part of Lee's duties as commander of the Union Army would include invading his own home and people. The ethical bottom line for Lee was the idea that a person does not invade his own home and people. Rather, he defends them if they are attacked. Therefore, Robert E. Lee became a general in the Confederate Army, not because he supported the Confederate cause, but because he felt morally obliged to defend his own home. I cite this example because of its dramatic presentation of the depth of ethical conflict that can arise and because of Lee's clear understanding of where his ethical priorities lay. Defense of his home and family was a moral value that Lee could not violate and that he was willing to die for as a consequence.

Determination of what one's summum bonum is becomes complicated because some people have many very high values that they believe in. In these cases, it becomes difficult to answer what the highest value is. For some, there may be no single highest value. The key issue is that practitioners need to seriously face the issue of the summum bonum and become conscious of what, if anything, these could be. Once this level of consciousness has been attained, then one can be prepared to rationally examine that value. Refusal to critically reason about one's summum bonum can easily degenerate into a form of thoughtless ethical fundamentalism. Just because a value is fundamental to one's ethical posture need not imply a thoughtless, uncritical application of that value to real problems.

Once the practitioner has become conscious of his or her summum bonum, a very effective way of submitting it to intellectual testing is by comparing it with rival sources of the highest good. I have argued that the problem with Utilitarianism is that it may justify too much. A problem with the Kantian Categorical Imperative is that it may justify too little. The point is that any highest good should be examined for areas where it is weak. The competing sources of the highest good not only include utility and duty, but also love, power, the civil law, and other concepts. All of these can be used to test the adequacy of one's belief in a summum bonum.

The methodological application of the summum bonum has been discussed in terms of ethical concepts and abstractions. This is the typical way in which philosophical ethics is done. There has been some fascinating research done recently by an educational psychologist that has a different methodological approach. Carol Gilligan has studied the different ways in which men and women approach moral dilemmas. According to Gilligan's research findings, on the confrontation of ethical problems, most men immediately cast the problem in terms of competing abstract values. They then proceed logically to wrestle with the conflicts of value and try to find a reasonable solution to the issue. Women, on the other hand, tend to interpret the problem in terms of the specific people involved in the case. The women tend to see the ethical conflicts in terms of relationships not abstractions. Gilligan cites the example of the Heinz case. Heinz is a young man who is married. His wife is dying from an illness. Heinz and his wife are poor and they cannot afford to pay the high price for a life-saving drug. The druggist is unwilling to give them the drug. Would Heinz be morally justified in stealing the drug?

According to Gilligan, males and females respond to this case very differently. Jake (the male voice) and Amy (the female voice) answer the question using different methodologies. Jake's response to the morality of the Heinz case

Chapter One / Ethical Theory

is summarized by Gilligan:

Fascinated by the power of logic, this eleven-year-old boy locates truth in math, which, he says, is "the only thing that is totally logical." Consideringthe moral dilemma to be "sort of like a math problem with humans," he sets it up as an equation and proceeds to work out the solution. Since his solution is rationally derived, he assumes that anyone following reason would arrive at the same conclusion and thus that a judge would also consider stealing to be the right thing for Heinz to do. [17]   Amy, on the other hand, responds to the Heinz case differently.

Instead, seeing a world comprised of relationships rather than of people standing alone, a world that coheres through human connection rather than through systems of rules, she finds the puzzle in the dilemma to lie in the failure of the druggist to respond to the wife. Saying that "it is not right for someone to die when their life could be saved," she assumes that if the druggist were to see the consequences of his refusal to lower his price, he would realize that "he should just give it to the wife and then have the husband pay back the money later."

- and later -

Both children thus recognize the need for agreement but see it mediated in different ways - he impersonally through systems of logic and law, she personally through communication in relationships. [18]

Jake wants to figure out the logic of the case and Amy wants to go talk to the druggist. Jake extracts himself from the case and Amy wants to stay within the case.

This is not the time to present a detailed critique of Carol Gilligan's work. I cite it as a good example of the methodological differences that can be applied to ethical issues in experiential education. Gilligan is not talking about gender exclusively, but about a difference in approach to moral problems. It is arguable that what is needed, methodologically, is the inclusion of both approaches to moral problems that arise. Every case that presents itself to practitioners will involve both abstractions **and** relationships in conflict. In the search for the summum bonum, it is useful to keep in mind whether the highest good is rooted in an abstract philosophical concept, within the context of human relationships, or in both.

Most experiential education practitioners work within a school, a program, or some other type of institutional setting. Something that is helpful in presenting a methodology is to pay attention to the values that the organization holds out as goals to be attained. This is formulated in terms of the "ends-means" distinction.

When asked what the chief goal of education is in the United States, educational policy makers frequently reply that preparation for participation in a democracy is a chief goal. This follows the Jeffersonian ideal of an educated citizenry being the key element for a democracy to function. An end value, then, is democratic participation. The next question is, "What are the means used to achieve this end?" According to John Dewey, it is vital that end values must be present in the means used to achieve those values. I have written elsewhere about Dewey's insistence that end values must be operative in means:

This can be made clear by an example from education. Educators are constantly asserting the idea that education should be an intellectual preparation for living in a democratic society. This preparation can be seen as an end towards which education strives. But, all too often, the actual practices of education and the means of education have little or nothing to do with anything even remotely resembling the democratic process. This results in a conceptual and practical split between the end (i.e., democratic participation) and the means (i.e., lack of democratic participation). [19]

If the ends of a program and the means that the program uses are dysjunctive, then there results what I call "valuational schizophrenia." To say that one values democratic ideals as an end and then to proceed to deny these very values in the educational means used is to fall into valuational schizophrenia.

This means that, methodologically speaking, practitioners ought carefully to check out if they are being faithful to the values that they hold as good. For a practitioner to hold out an end value of increased personal responsibility by students and then to deny students any meaningful opportunities for exercise of personal responsibility is to violate the very end value that was espoused as good. Put succinctly, the precept is to ask oneself, "Do I practice what I preach?"

An important consideration in the development of an ethical methodology is the place of historical context and historical lessons. Ethical issues arise within a context of some sort and every context presupposes a history that preceded the context. I think it is crucial that practitioners become familiar with lessons learned from history that may be germane to the specific cases in which they find themselves. In many cases, the lessons of history may be sufficiently clear to render the problematic case no longer an issue. The use of the word "history" should be seen as wide and flexible. Practitioners working within an institutional setting ought to become knowledgeable about the history of that institution. Such knowledge can give valuable clues about how its practitioners in the past have dealt with ethical issues. I hasten to add that paying close attention to historical precedents can easily degenerate into a thoughtless following of precedent. I am not suggesting that just because ethical matters were handled a certain way in the past that they should necessarily be handled that way in the future. One might look at the historical precedents and

Chapter One / Ethical Theory

judge that those actions were flawed. My point is not a "slave-like" devotion to history. Rather, history can be seen as providing extremely valuable information to the practitioners making moral judgments.

Part of the use of history in an ethical methodology is to pay attention to ethical concepts that have survived the test of time. Before making a judgment or decision, it is prudent to seek the counsel of the masters of old. While the old counselors are not physically available to offer advice, their surviving ethical methodologies can often be used. Earlier in this chapter I cited several of the most influential ethical figures in history including Biblical sources, Plato, Aristotle, Kant, and John Stuart Mill. It seems clear to me that all of these sources offer valuable ethical guidance. Before deciding to make ethical judgement "A," the decision maker might ask what the Kantian Categorical Imperative would imply. This could be brought up against the Utilitarian Calculus or the Ten Commandments. Granted, these different approaches to ethics are often in conflict and simply comparing them to a Utilitarian approach to a Biblical approach may not suffice to solve the problem at hand. The point is not simple solutions. Rather, greater clarity of thought can be obtained by paying attention to major ethical theories as they apply to a given ethical problem. It should be clear by this point in the book that I oppose a slavish, mindless devotion to any single historical source of ethics. Refusing to mindlessly adhere to a particular ethical methodology, however, need not rule out gaining greater insight into the ethical complexities of a particular case. It is my view that in order to be intellectually honest, the ethical decision maker is obliged to pay attention to the guidance offered by historical sources.

Once a historical perspective has been obtained, it is useful for the ethicist to think as much like a scientist as possible. This means that a practitioner about to make an ethical judgment should project possible effects of that judgement in the future. Scientists formulate hypotheses in order for them be tested in the future. Knowledge of the future is tentative until the future becomes the present and then the past. Nevertheless, future effects can be estimated and probable effects can be ascertained. If I make ethical decision A, then what might result? If I make decision B, then what might result? The point is that by attempting to reason out the result of a given decision can help test whether or not I really want or ought to make that decision.

Methodologically, it is often tempting to try to find a single aspect of a complex decision-making process and use that one aspect while ignoring the others. Philosopher Alfred North Whitehead calls this "the fallacy of misplaced concreteness." In reference to this fallacy, Whitehead writes:

This fallacy consists in neglecting the degree of abstraction involved when an actual entity is considered merely so far as it exemplifies certain categories of thought. There are aspects of actualities which are simply ignored so long as we restrict thought to these categories. Thus the success of a philosophy is to be measured by its comparative avoidance of this fallacy, when thought is restricted within its categories. [20]

Applied to an ethical methodology, the fallacy of misplaced concreteness is a warning to those making ethical decisions not to neglect "the degree of abstraction involved" when judging a complicated situation. There are many methodological influences to consider and it is a mistake to fail to be cognizant of these influences.

Finally, after all is said and done, decisions still must be made. The teacher on the spot does not always have the luxury of exhaustive, methodologically correct analysis. This is mainly a function of time. Time will not stop so that the decision maker can rationally reflect on all of the complexities of every case which presents itself. The moment of decision is a moment that can be quite lonely for the teacher or instructor. Whatever decision is made, there always exists the possibility it will be wrong. This is a fact of life for any person concerned about doing the morally right thing. This possibility must be faced and embraced as inherently bound up with ethical decision making. Realization of one's fallibility, however, need not lead to paralysis of action. Martin Luther King was plagued by doubts about the rightness of his actions. Yet he acted. It is that rare combination of self-doubt, coupled with a willingness to act on the best of one's understanding of the morally right path, that makes for heroes. It also makes for tragedy at times. Experiential education practitioners have no less difficult a task than did King. The issues are the same. Only the settings change.

Belay practice is over. It is time to get up to the climbing area.

Endnotes / Chapter 1

1. Aristotle, Nicomachean Ethics, Book I, Chapter 3, in The Basic Works of Aristotle, Richard McKean, ed. (New York: Random House, 1941), 936.

2. Alfred North Whitehead, Process and Reality, ed. David Ray Griffin and Donald W. Sherburne (New York: The Free Press, 1978), 7.

3. Plato, Theaetetus, 152A3. in Plato: The Collected Dialogues (Princeton University Press, 1969), 856.

4. Dave Hume, A Treatise of Human Nature , ed. L. A. Selby-Bigge (Oxford University Press, 1978), 468-469.

Chapter One / Ethical Theory

5. Plato, Republic (Book 7, 517b-c5) in Plato: The Collected Dialogues (Princeton: Princeton University Press, 1969), 749-750.

6. "Exodus 20:20" in The New Oxford Annotated Bible (New York: Oxford University Press, 1973), 93.

7. Proverbs 3:5-8, 772.

8. John Stuart Mill "Utilitarianism" in Ethical Theories, ed. A. I. Melden (Englewood Cliffs: Prentice-Hall, 1967), 391.

9. Mill, "Utilitarianism", 395.

10. Henry Sidgwick, The Methods of Ethics, 7th ed. (Chicago: University of Chicago Press, 1907), 8.

11. Morton White, Science and Sentiment in America (New York: Oxford University Press, 1972), 93.

12. Exodus 20:16.

13. Immanuel Kant, Foundations of the Metaphysics of Morals (Indianapolis: Bobbs-Merrill, 1980), 16.

14. Kant, 17.

15. Kant, 33.

16. Kant, 39

17. Carol Gilligan, A Different Voice (Cambridge: Harvard University Press, 1982), 26, 27.

18. Gilligan, 29.

19. Jasper S. Hunt, Jr. "On the Applicability of the Epistemologies and Theories of Value of Alfred North Whitehead and John Dewey to the Development of an Experience-Based Teacher Education Program" (Ph.D. Diss. University of Colorado, 1983), 107.

20. Alfred North Whitehead, Process and Reality, ed. Griffin and Sherburne (New York: Macmillan, 1978), 7, 8.

Chapter Two

Risk-Benefit Analysis

During the national conference of the Association for Experiential Education in Santa Fe, New Mexico, Fall, 1980, I had a very interesting experience. I had the golden opportunity of sitting in the cab of a pickup truck with Paul Petzoldt for 45 minutes, while we drove to the nearest watering hole to go dancing. I had never met Paul Petzoldt before that truck trip. However, by that stage in my career as an experiential educator, I had safely instructed several thousand student-days worth of high adventure activities. I was proud of my safety record but I was beginning to wonder when "the big accident" would finally happen. Sitting in the cab next to the legendary mountaineer and educator, I figured it would be a good time to get his opinion on this subject. So, I asked him, "What advice do you have for someone at my stage of professional development who is worried about losing a student to serious injury or death? You know, when will the law of averages catch up with me?" Petzoldt looked at me with his bushy eyebrows pulled into a frown and in a booming voice growled, "Are you a **fool**?"

I replied, slightly irritated by the tone of his question, "No, I am not a fool." "Well," he said, "If you aren't a **fool**, then you will never lose anyone, I don't care how many student-days worth of experience you have!"

I have thought about that conversation many, many times in the ensuing years. Something about Petzoldt's reply to my question did not sit right. On the one hand, I **knew** I wasn't a fool. On the other hand, knowing that I wasn't a fool did not leave my original question adequately answered.

One could go in two different directions from this point. If it is true that not being a fool and, hence, being an instructor with good judgment, suffices for the elimination of the possibility of student death or injury, then the issue of risk becomes solvable by having nonfoolish instructors. Petzoldt's reply to my question presupposed that instructor judgment was the independent variable operating in the risk issue. If the issue of risk, therefore, converts to an issue of instructor judgment, a whole other set of issues emerge. The focus then shifts to the preparation and training of instructors who are not foolish. In a sense the original issue (risk) has disappeared and has been replaced by another issue (instructor training).

It took me several years to figure out that the reason I was not satisfied by Paul Petzoldt's reply to my question was that the reply completely evaded the root issue I was wrestling with. My concern was with what mountaineers call "objective risk." By risk I meant aspects of nature that were beyond the instructors' control and that operated regardless of the good judgment of the instructor. My presupposition was that even an instructor with the wisdom of a King Solomon might encounter an unpredictable act of nature that defies her good judgment, her lack of foolishness, and results in the death or injury of a student.

The ethical issue that raises its head, therefore, is whether it is morally acceptable to expose students to educational activities that might very well harm or kill them in order to achieve good educational ends. I am not talking about instructor judgment here. I am talking about risk that transcends sound instructor judgment.

This can well be illustrated from an example not from education. Every time we, as a culture, decide to pave a stretch of highway, we know as a matter of empirically verifiable fact, that a number of people will die in traffic accidents while traveling along that stretch of highway. Granted, we do everything within reason to minimize the risk. We employ expert traffic engineers and construction companies to design and build the highway. We prohibit drivers from traveling too fast. We certify and license drivers. We pass laws against driving while intoxicated. We inspect automobiles for safety features, etc., etc. In short, we do everything within reason to minimize the risk, but we cannot possibly **eliminate** the risk completely. In spite of our best efforts we know that people will die on that highway. Yet we build it anyway. The ethical question that emerges is how can we morally justify building highways on which we know people will die. Do not build the highway and no one will die on a highway that does not exist. This is beyond dispute. Many, many arguments can be articulated to justify the building of the highway in spite of its harm and death potential. I think the ethical issue with building highways is quite similar to the chief issue of this chapter.

Ultimately, we justify the building of the highway because the benefits of having highways outweigh the risks involved. I call this the "argument from benefit." Supporters of the argument from benefit do not quarrel with the fact that people will be hurt and killed on the highway. They accept this fact but argue that the benefits justify the risks.

For experiential educators, especially those engaged in the high adventure wing of experiential education, the issue of risks and benefits must be faced head on. This leads directly into the second direction one can take to the issue. Rather than engage in a form of psychological denial, as my first alternative does, the experiential educator can simply accept the fact that some students may die. Once this move is made, the problem becomes one of ethical justification of the educational use of risky activities.

Before proceeding with this issue further, the very first step that must be taken is that I must make a clear, unequivocal, and emphatic statement. **I am not talking about reckless risk. I am talking about risks that exist as inherent to the environments in which we conduct our activities.** Imagine for a moment, if you will, the creation of the ideal adventure-based experiential educator. She is not foolish. She has stunningly superb judgment. Her technical skills are world class. In short, she is the perfect instructor. The issue this chapter is concerned with is the risk the students of this mythically perfect instructor would face in a wilderness environment. The question is this: Can valid arguments be put forth that ethically defend the impelling of students into inherently risky situations? If no convincing arguments can be found, then experiential education activities that involve risk must be condemned as immoral, and these activities should cease being used.

One way to proceed is to go back to my "argument from benefit." As applied to experiential education, the argument from benefit proceeds by admitting the reality of risk, but justifies exposing students to risky activities because of the benefits that will be gained. Thus, in a situation of low risk, but high benefit, it might be easy to convince someone that the risk, while real, is nevertheless very small and that the possible benefits are so high that a reasonable person would take this risk. This is precisely the way the highway construction example works. Granted, there is a risk every time I proceed on that highway in my automobile. However, I judge every time I get behind the wheel that the risk is so minimal and the benefits are so great, that I will go ahead and drive my car, while exercising great care and caution in order to minimize my risk.

It is arguable that what is needed is a risk-benefit calculation that will resolve the ethical problem at hand. In a perfect application of the risk-benefit model, we could develop two independent sets of numbers. One set of numbers would be the risk numbers. These numbers would indicate the level of risk of harm of any given activity. The other set of numbers would be the benefit numbers. A sort of mathematical proportion could be developed. In other words, suppose activity A had a risk level of 80 on a scale of 1-100, with 100 representing the

Chapter Two / Risk-Benefit Analysis

highest risk. However, activity A would have a benefit of, say, 10 on a scale of 1-100 with 100 representing the highest benefit. It would be easy to reason that since the risk is very high (80) and the benefit is very low (10), that, therefore, the ethical thing to do is not to use this activity as an educational tool. If the risk-benefit calculation were the way to go in this matter, then we as a profession could assign numerical cutoff points to guide us. We could even develop logarithmic-type tables of risks and benefits, publish those tables, give them to field instructors with cut-off points indicated and thereby solve our ethical problem in a neat and tidy fashion. There is something nutty and absurd about this solution to the problem.

To think that we would ever successfully quantify risks and benefits would be to deny the complexity and fluidity of the physical world in which we operate and the variability of human responses to what constitutes an acceptable risk. On the world side, imagine the variations of risk that a given snow slope in the mountains presents. A low avalanche danger slope can be transformed, with a few hours of high wind and snowfall, into an extremely high-risk slope. This does not mean that no natural environments can be reliably predicted for risk potential. It just means that many of the natural environments routinely used by experiential educators cannot be predicted precisely. The problem of variability of risk potential exists in most natural environments.

While the dynamic nature of the natural world presents problems for the quantification of risk, the human perception and understanding of what constitutes an acceptable risk offers an even more problematic issue. As J.E.J. Altham puts it:

One of the more evident facts in this area is that people's attitudes towards risk and uncertainty vary greatly. To some people, in some circumstances, the consciousness of risk has positive value. To others in the same circumstances, the consciousness of risk may be unpleasant. What gives one some pleasurable excitement gives another the pain of anxiety. A person may be temperamentally risk averse or risk loving.[1]

Thus, the problem of the quantification of the objectivity of risk is difficult at best, both in terms of the reality of risk itself and in terms of the human, subjective, responses to risk.

The quantification of benefits is even more elusive than the quantification of risks. This is where the force of the subjectivist ethical position presents a compelling case. In order to quantify a benefit mathematically, there must exist some objective source of benefit. But, the concept of a benefit is quite subjective. The 5.11 rock climber maintains that she derives great existential benefit from exposing herself to high risks. How can one possibly attach a numerical value to this person's claim to gain existential benefit? If the concept of benefit is strongly influenced by subjective factors, then the possibility of reaching mathematical certainty about what counts as a given amount of benefit is remote. Thus, my conclusion is that the risk-benefit mathematical calculation is not the best way for experiential educators to proceed on this ethical issue.

I was hired as an instructor by the Northwest Outward Bound School (now called Pacific Crest Outward Bound School) during the Spring of 1974. During staff training, the director of the school, William H. (Bill) Byrd gave us a talk about safety and risk management in the field. In those days field instructors had a great deal of freedom in determining course structure. For instance, during peak climbs we were free to select the routes we would use with the students. During his talk, Bill broached the subject of taking students up a route that presented a higher level of objective danger than another less risky route up the same mountain. The question arose about how we should go about making these decisions. (Of course, the assumption was we would never take students up a route that was beyond the instructor's or students' technical competence.) Byrd suggested that a key question we field instructors should ask ourselves was "What is the educational significance of this decision?" In other words, was there any educationally important factor to be gained by doing the more risky route? If we could not clearly articulate an educational benefit to be gained by the riskier route, then it might well be better to stick with the less risky standard routes.

There is some ethical mileage to be gained from Bill Byrd's advice. One of the problems with risk-benefit analysis based upon a mathematical calculation was the problem of defining what constituted a benefit. Here Byrd has defined benefit in terms of an educational benefit. In other words, it could be argued that a risky activity in experiential education is justified if sufficient educational benefit can be demonstrated.

Talk of educational benefits turns rapidly to talk of educational goals. An educational benefit makes sense only in terms of the goals of a given educational enterprise. For instance, if my goal is to introduce beginning students to mountaineering in order to increase positive self-concept, I might calculate educational goals very differently than if I am teaching advanced students who are headed for a Himalayan expedition. I might very well be able to accomplish the goals of the beginning students without exposing them to much objective risk. If that is the case, I would be hard put to justify impelling the beginners into the more dangerous situation. On the other hand, the future Himalayan climbers might need additional objective risks in order to prepare them properly for the danger they will encounter in the Himalayas. Morally, I could be condemned for exposing the beginners to too much risk and condemned for not exposing the advanced students to enough risk. The point here is that the educational worth of risks can only be evaluated in terms of educational goals, which in turn influence whether the risk-use is moral or immoral.

The move to evaluate the ethical significance of risks and benefits in terms of educational goals leads into what I believe to be one of the key issues operative here. It has often been argued that the ideal situation is one in which the benefits of impelling students into risky situations can be accomplished without having the situation be really risky at all. A distinction can be made between **objective** and **perceived** risk. Ethically, it can be argued that if the educational goals can be accomplished by using situations that are not in fact risky, then that is the way to go, rather than using methods that are really risky in order to accomplish the exact same goals.

For readers not familiar with the distinction between objective and perceived risk, some amplification is in order. I have already discussed objective risk in the opening of this chapter. However, perceived risk is a very different matter. I have a picture on my office wall of a student doing a high rappel. Faculty members not knowledgeable about experiential education come into my office and marvel at the daring-do represented by this picture. "Wow!" they exclaim, "That looks wild. You experiential educators are really big risk-takers!" What they do not know is that the student is tied into ropes that will hold several thousand pounds of weight; he is wearing a very expensive helmet; he is anchored to solid rock; and on top of all that, he has a completely independently-rigged backup belay system, just in case something were to happen. Yet, to the uninformed, the high rappel appears to be quite risky. The high rappel pictured on my office wall is perceptually very risky and objectively very safe.

The point is that if the educational goals can be reached via the perceived risk route, then those who would use higher risk activities **in order to achieve the same goals** are faced with a troubling, difficult task.

In a sense, the move to shift the focus of the risk discussion from objective risk to perceived risk is very similar to the move at the beginning of the chapter to shift the focus to instructor judgment. This move presupposes that perceived risk is, in fact, objectively safe. But is it? Take my example of the high rappel again. If asked why am I using that activity as an educational means, I could reply, "Because, it is actually very safe but it looks dangerous. It is in the looking dangerous that I gain the educational worth of the experience." But is that high rappel really only perceptually, subjectivistically, risky? Suppose those solid rock anchors were to somehow give way, both at the anchor point of the rappel ropes and at the belay point. Suppose an electrical storm were to blow in while a student was frozen with fear half way down. Suppose the student's rope dislodged a rock above his head and it came crashing down on top of him? Suppose the student's hair clip were to break and he got his hair tangled up in the descending device? Suppose a rattlesnake were to bite him while his leg rests on a ledge? Suppose, Suppose, Suppose. Many events could happen to shatter the illusion that the high rappel is actually safe and only perceptually risky.

The key issue in this example is that the high rappel is neither completely objectively risky nor is it completely subjectively risky. Objectively, many things could happen to cause harm or death to a student while on the rappel. However, there is great strength in the argument that, in terms of probabilities, the major risk factors have been eliminated or minimized.

Thus a vital, pervasive tension emerges that is of great ethical significance for experiential education. **We put our students in situations that could harm or kill them, but we do everything reasonable in our power to prevent harm.** The potential for harm is inherent in the environment, because it is a natural environment. It is the environment that is risky, not the program. In referring to the natural environment as an educational tool Willi Unsoeld once said:

It is real, real enough to kill you. And that impresses the kids. You get the students out there; if it's real enough to kill you, it's got to be real. And what is real is relevant. [2]

The beginning point of the tension lies in the objectivity of the nature of the environment. However, the other side of the tension rests in a commitment to do everything possible to avoid letting that environment hurt the students. Willi Unsoeld again has a comment on this side of the tension:

You emphasize safety in a high risk operation. You emphasize safety, but **you don't kill the risk.** *You emphasize safety as a rational man's effort at survival, but we're going to go right ahead and stick our head in the noose...that's the game. But we're going to be so careful in doing it, at the same time, and that delicate balance, you know, I think it just has to be transmitted, all the time. We don't do anything stupid. There's enough out there to get you anyhow.* [3]

Unsoeld's quote provides one of the possible responses that could be given in answer to the demand for a moral justification for impelling students into risky situations. The move can be made that acknowledges the inherent risk involved with natural settings, while at the same time vigorously asserting a commitment to safety and eliminating needless risk for the students. This is where Paul Petzoldt's concern about not being foolish and exercising good judgment becomes useful.

However, it is vital to realize here that the move at hand does not attempt a psychological denial of risk. It admits the reality of risk but it seeks to minimize it. The tension that I mentioned earlier resides in the "delicate balance" that

Chapter Two / Risk-Benefit Analysis

Unsoeld referred to. On the one hand we "don't kill the risk" and, on the other hand, "we don't do anything stupid."

One argument I have heard over the years in favor of higher objective risk activities is that these higher risk activities increase the happiness level of the instructional staff. The phenomenon of staff members becoming bored with teaching activities that at one time were exciting but are currently boring is very common. Frankly, I think this argument is quite weak. It is weak because it considers the psychological well being of the staff members as a relevant variable when considering the health and lives of students. It seems clear that increasing the objective risk of harm to students in order to save burned-out staff from boredom is unethical in the extreme. It is arguable that a staff member who is so bored with her job that she cannot appreciate the risk-experience of the students, should simply leave that job and do something else.

The original issue of this chapter has yet to be adequately addressed. One might well retort that since we cannot completely eliminate the risks because of the nature of the environmental settings, that we have not provided a convincing justification for using those risky environments in the first place. Someone morally opposed to the use of inherently risky environments as an educational tool might well not be satisfied by the sort of responses offered by Petzoldt and Unsoeld.

The reply to this most fundamental ethical question must be firmly rooted in the very nature of experiential education itself. The presupposition behind the demand for risk-free education is patently false. It is false because risk-free education is a contradiction in terms. Education without risk is no more possible than having water without moisture. Notice that a vital and dramatic shift of emphasis has taken place in the reply. I am no longer talking about the adventure-based wing of experiential education, I am talking about all experiential education.

Few would disagree with the assertion that a chief goal of education is to encourage people to think rather than go through life mindlessly. Fundamental to the application of thought to the world is the impossibility of complete certainty of outcome. For if the outcome of thought were completely known in advance, there would be no need for thought at all. Thinking implies taking a risk. As John Dewey says about this matter:

It also follows that all thinking involves a risk. Certainty cannot be guaranteed in advance. The invasion of the unknown is of the nature of an adventure; we cannot be sure in advance. The conclusions of thinking, till confirmed by the event, are, accordingly, more or less tentative or hypothetical. Their dogmatic assertion as final is unwarranted, short of the issue, in fact.[4]

Thinking implies taking a risk because we only have a need to think about that which we do not know. What we do not know is by its very nature indeterminate. Without indeterminancy there can be no thought. Without thought there can be no educationally valid experience. Therefore, there is a vital link between education and the risk inherent in the process of thought itself. **It is our duty as educators to encourage our students to take the risk of thought.**

Therefore, the ethical table can be turned on those who would demand risk-free education. That demand is tantamount to demanding that we ask our students to stop thinking. Who is being more unethical here, the one who takes calculated risks or the one who would kill education itself by killing the risk inherent in thinking?

The educator who uses the high rappel is consciously impelling her students into a risky situation. So is the science teacher who uses chemicals in a laboratory experiment. So is the English teacher who sends her students out to do cultural journalism projects. So is the teacher who encourages her students to play sports. So is the teacher who urges her social studies students to question the values of their immediate environment. So is the medical school teacher who insists that her students examine sick patients. The point here is that the issue of risk in education is not limited to those in the adventure-based wing of experiential education. It is inherent in the very nature of education in general.

Once this move is made in response to the demand for an ethical justification for the use of risk in experiential education, great progress has been made. For the idea of risk has at least gotten its foot in the door. The opening has been made, not in terms of an abstract justification imposed from on high but, instead, in terms of the very nature of education.

A vital issue emerges at this point, for the argument has come full circle. Once risk is admitted into the educational arena, the original problem emerges about how much risk for how much educational benefit is morally justified. I have already suggested the impossibility of a facile answer to this in terms of a certain mathematical calculation of risk and benefit. However, it still seems reasonable to argue that risk and benefit are not completely elusive terms.

This is where the power of empirical knowledge is very useful for the ethicist. As much as possible, the defender of the use of risk for educational benefits should try to clearly demonstrate the benefits that can be obtained from the use of risk. If it can be shown empirically that increased self-concept results from the use of activities such as the high rappel, then the defender of the use of this activity has a much more convincing argument than if no proof can be given. Again, reasonable people will probably agree that a relatively high benefit makes the use of a relatively low risk more acceptable than if no benefit

Chapter Two / Risk-Benefit Analysis

can be shown at all. Programmatically, this puts the discipline of the compilation of data and other empirical research methods on the educator's shoulders. Information must be collected and made available, both in terms of the risks and in terms of the benefits.

The issues raised in Chapter 1 have been operating throughout this chapter, although not all of that language has been utilized here. The distinction between ethical subjectivism and ethical objectivism has been used. We have seen that both the subjectivity and the objectivity of risks and benefits are relevant to the ethical issues at hand. I have attempted to show that subjective and objective factors involved in the risk/benefit analysis are not at all separable.

The demand that risk be completely eliminated from experiential education is clearly an example of nonconsequentialist ethical thought at work in a practical application. The summum bonum of this train of thought is safety. The reasoning process is that since safety is regarded as the highest good, anything that compromises safety with risk is clearly immoral. The nonconsequentialist argues that the ends (educational benefit) do not morally justify the means (risk) used to gain that benefit. The act itself (impelling students into a risky situation) becomes wrong because it compromises the summum bonum (safety). Thus, a rigid moral barrier is erected between students and the use of risk as an educational tool.

Consequentialist ethical theory is also operative here. The consequentialist holds the concept of educational benefit as the summum bonum. Whether or not a given act of risk-use in education is morally justified can only be determined, post facto, in terms of the amount of benefit produced. The means, therefore, are not in themselves moral or immoral. The means become moral or immoral only in terms of the normative standard of educational benefit.

It should be clear that to approach the issue of risk and benefit in education, armed only with either a consequentialist or a nonconsequentialist attitude, is to invite trouble. The nonconsequentialist would, arguably, severely restrict the use of risk as an educational tool. This could well eliminate the gain of great educational benefits to many students. On the other hand, the consequentialist might well allow too much risk because of the great benefit obtained for many students. As I said in Chapter 1, the problem with consequentialism in general is that it may justify too much. The problem with nonconsequentialism is that it may well not justify enough. Thus, the rival summum bonums are in conflict. Safety and educational benefit cannot both be the summum bonum. It seems clear that either of these two, if allowed to stand alone, will lead to problems. Practitioners therefore are left with a built-in tension in their professional lives. They embrace risky activities and they embrace a commitment to safety. It would be comforting for many practitioners if a final ethical answer could be given here. I do not have the final answer other than to urge practitioners to acknowledge the tension and use it as a source of moral reflection. It is enough to point out this conflict in this book without attempting a final resolution.

Endnotes / Chapter 2

1. J. E. J. Altham, "Ethics of Risk," Proceedings of the Aristotelian Society. 84 (Summer 1984), 24.

2. William F. Unsoeld, "Outdoor Education". Lecture presented at The Evergreen State College, Spring, 1977. Tape #2 (Olympia: Copyright 1979 by Jolene Unsoeld).

3. William F. Unsoeld, "Outdoor Education". Lecture presented to Charles Wright Academy, November 19, 1976 (Olympia: Copyright 1979 by Jolene Unsoeld).

4. John Dewey, Democracy and Education (New York: Macmillan, 1916), 148.

Chapter Three

Informed Consent

Throughout the discussion of risks and benefits in experiential education, a key issue was presupposed as settled and taken for granted. I assumed in Chapter 2 that the ethical issue was chiefly that of risks and benefits and that the participants and staff members were fully informed about potential risks and benefits. This is a dangerous assumption to make. It is dangerous because it may be a false assumption and false assumptions give rise to troublesome conclusions. Although as practitioners we may believe that our students are aware of possible risks, we can be mistaken in our beliefs. If we are mistaken in our beliefs, we may be treading on ethically shaky ground in our use of risk as an educational tool. The morality of using risk is strongly influenced by whether or not the student knew what he was getting himself into before he got there.

Broadly speaking, I shall refer to this issue of knowing what one is getting oneself into as **informed consent**. A great deal has been written about informed consent in the field of medical ethics. It will be very helpful for the discussion here to make use of ideas derived from medical ethics as they apply to experiential education. In a discussion of the role of informed consent in medical ethics, M.D. Kirby writes:

The principle of informed consent requires that health professionals, before any diagnostic or therapeutic procedure is carried out which may have any reasonable possibility of harm to the patient, explain to the patient what is involved in order to secure the understanding consent of the patient to proceed. **An informed consent is that consent which is obtained after the patient has been adequately instructed about the ratio of risk and benefit involved in the procedure as compared to alternative procedures or no treatment at all.** [1]

A careful application of the standard of informed consent contained in this quote to the field of experiential education presents many problems and challenges. It should be obvious immediately that the words "adequately instructed about the ratio of risk and benefit" direct us to the complexities raised in Chapter 2 about the problem of quantifying of risks and benefits in experiential education.

Suppose I go to a physician and am diagnosed as having strep throat. I am told that the treatment of choice is penicillin. I am warned that an allergic reaction to the penicillin is possible but not probable. I am also warned that if left untreated, strep can lead to severe heart damage. The ratio of risk to benefit is a rather simple one for an intelligent layperson to understand. The benefit is clear and so is the risk. Therefore, informed consent is easily obtained.

Suppose I want to improve my low self-concept by attending a three-week wilderness program. (I have already established the impossibility of an exact mathematical calculation which will tell me exactly what the risks are when entering a wilderness area.) The program I am about to attend cannot tell me with the same precision that the physician can, exactly what the risk side of the ratio is. However, the program can tell me **something** about the risks involved in terms of the program's overall safety record; its adherence to a safety policy; the qualifications of the staff it hires; the general risks presented by the environment I will be in and so forth. The point is that the issue of informing participants, while difficult and complex, is not completely elusive in experiential education. It is important not to fall into the fallacious reasoning process of thinking that just because risks are not completely quantifiable, therefore, informed consent is impossible. **Informed consent need not be predicated upon a completely quantified analysis of risk.**

The issue of evaluating the possible benefits attendant to participating in an experiential education program is also difficult to inform someone about. While the physician can tell me with great confidence of the benefits of being cured of a strep infection, the experiential educator cannot make such unequivocal assurances about the benefits of attending his program. Granted, if I attend the program in order to improve my self-concept, I may in fact emerge confident and made whole. However, unless the people offering the program can know beforehand with a high degree of assurance that I will improve my self-concept, it would be highly unethical for them to lie to me about that which they do not know. However, just as risk-consent need not be predicated upon completely quantified information, so too with benefit-consent. Although I cannot be told for sure that I will improve my self-concept, nevertheless, I can be told that many people have received such positive benefits. Again, the impossibility of **certainty** of benefit need not rule out being informed about **possibilities** of benefit.

It should be pointed out here that the analogy to medicine and informed

Chapter Three / Informed Consent

consent may not be handled easily on the medical side either. In reference to the difficulties of obtaining informed consent, even in a medical setting, Tom Beauchamp and Leroy Walters have written:

*What is the proper meaning of informed consent? The **consent** element is relatively unproblematic, but what is it to give **informed** consent, as distinct from either partially informed or uninformed consent? Physicians are hardly in a position to give patients a course in medicine, as a way of explaining their problem. But how can patients make an informed decision if they incompletely comprehend their medical condition?* [2]

Strictly speaking, in order for me to give true **informed** consent to anything, I must possess as much information as is available about that to which I am consenting. But in order to have such complete information in a medical situation, I would have to attend medical school, complete a residency and be up on the latest research in order to give informed consent. This is obviously an absurd situation and an absurd remedy to the problem. Similarly, to give truly informed consent in an experiential education situation, I must first become an expert in experiential education practices before I can give my consent. Thus, the strict criteria for informed consent reduces to an absurdity rapidly, even in a medical situation, which at first glance appeared relatively easy.

I think the solution to this dilemma resides in refusing to accept either that we must have completely informed consent or dismiss the possibility of informed consent altogether. If we do not accept either of these two extremes, then what are we to accept? Beauchamp and Walters argue for the adaptation of the notion of the "reasonable man" criterion:

*In confronting this and other problems, some courts have adopted the standard of the 'reasonable man': the physician must have informed the patient to the extent that **any reasonable man** (or woman) would have to be informed in order to make a decision about his (or her) case.* [3]

Becoming informed about risks and benefits need not be an all or nothing affair. The criterion of the reasonable man is useful for experiential educators because it allows for the possibility of gradations of becoming informed. I need not be completely informed in order to exercise my ability to reason about the possible risks and benefits in a given experiential education situation.

I expect that readers may raise the important question about what qualifies as a reasonable man acting reasonably in giving informed consent to a given activity. What is the difference between a reasonable man and an unreasonable man? A thorough answer to this question would require that I abandon this book and begin another one. However, a partial answer can be given here. John Dewey offers a definition of reason that is quite useful to the issue of informed consent. He writes:

Reasonableness or rationality is, according to the position here taken, as well as in its ordinary usage, an affair of the relation of means and consequences. In framing ends-in-view, it is unreasonable to set up those which have no connection with available means and without reference to the obstacles standing in the way of attaining the end.

-and later-

Rationality as an abstract conception is precisely the generalized idea of the means - consequence relation as such.[4]

To paraphrase Dewey: "exercising one's reasoning abilities means to have some awareness of the complex relationship of one's actions as partially determining future consequences." Thus, the rational person is one who can recognize the relationship between the ends one chooses and the means one chooses to pursue. One can easily substitute the words "risk" and "benefit" for means and ends. Risk is to means as benefit is to ends. A complete understanding of the means - ends relationship is not one which can be achieved apart from the complexities of the situations in which one finds oneself. It seems reasonable to conclude, therefore, that there will exist a correlation between the level of complexity presented by a means - ends situation and the level of certainty that can be attained by any reasonable person. Making the decision to proceed with open heart surgery necessarily involves one in a more complex means - ends situation than does the decision to accept treatment for strep throat. Similarly, the decision to attempt a mountaineering expedition for an educational benefit involves more complex reasoning in terms of informed consent than does the decision to collect wild flowers in a meadow. In a sense, the greater the complexity of risk and benefit involved, the greater the amount of reasonableness needed to give informed consent.

There is a deeper level of analysis to be addressed here that is very important for informed consent and for other issues in this book. The question should be faced about what is the moral principle which makes informed consent so important in the first place. One might argue that I am setting up a straw man in that I have given no arguments why informing people is better than not informing them. Why should an informed consent state of affairs receive moral approval, while a not-informed consent state of affairs is condemned?

The answer to this most basic question is rooted in the concept of **personal autonomy.** In a widely accepted definition of personal autonomy, Beauchamp and Childress have written;

Autonomy is a form of personal liberty of action where the individual determines his or her own course of action in accordance with a plan chosen by himself or herself. The autonomous person is one who not only deliberates about and chooses such plans but who is capable of acting on the basis of such deliberations just as a truly independent government has autonomous control of its territories, and policies.[5]

A person who is capable of acting autonomously is a person acting freely. Beauchamp and Childress root autonomy within a broader concept of **liberty**. In short, when one takes away another's autonomy, one is thereby restricting the person's liberty. If I am a reasonable person and I am deciding whether a given risky activity is worth the risk and I am **not informed** about what the risks are, then I am incapable of making a truly informed decision. The less information I have, the less I am acting autonomously. The less I act autonomously, the less I act from a state of liberty. Thus, my ignorance becomes a form of slavery. A slave gives no consent and has no claim to becoming informed. In the final analysis, the moral justification for informed consent is rooted in the idea that freedom is morally preferable to slavery. Restrict my access to information and you, thereby, restrict my freedom. (For another application of the issue of personal liberty in experiential education, readers should look at the chapter in this book on "Paternalism.")

This whole discussion of informed consent can be cast in terms of **non-consequentialist** versus **consequentialist** theories of ethics.

Following the methodology of the utilitarian form of consequentialism, the morality of informed consent in experiential education must be evaluated post facto to a given set of circumstances **if one is an act utilitarian.** (See Chapter 1 for the distinction between **act** and **rule** utilitarianism). Imagine that a potential student is contemplating attending an experiential education program that presents some objective risks. The student is suffering from extremely low self-esteem and has become nearly psychologically disabled due to a complete unwillingness to take any risks in his life. He is seeing a counselor about his problem and both the student and the counselor believe that great benefit can be gained by attending the experiential education program. The counselor decides, along with the director of the program, that given the exceptional safety record of the program, it would be best not to mention possible risks for fear of scaring the student away. Would this act of not thoroughly informing the student be morally right?

The act utilitarian, consequentialist ethicist might well argue that this judgment could be morally right if the decision were made with an eye toward maximizing a great good for that person. If after completing the course the student gains great benefit from the experience, an argument could be made that, based upon a utilitarian analysis of the specific act, not providing thorough information was morally justified.

On the other hand, a rule utilitarian would approach the case **very** differently. First, the rule utilitarian would refuse to focus in on the specific act in the first place. Rather, the concern would be with the **practice** of informed consent in general and its production of better rather than worse benefits. The rule utilitarian might conclude that the greatest good for the greatest number is best served by establishing a general rule that more happiness will result by always providing complete information to potential students.

However, the rule utilitarian could also go in the other direction and might argue that a rule could be established which would justify less than complete information in those cases which are similar to the one I just outlined. Thus, the good results of obtaining informed consent could be retained, while at the same time allowances could be made for cases that fell under the protection of a rule which permitted such exceptions.

An ethical nonconsequentialist would not evaluate the morality of the withholding of information post facto. Instead, the analysis would be focused on the act itself. From a Kantian perspective, the categorical imperative would be applied and the issue of the universalizability of the act itself would be raised.

In the situation just outlined, where great benefit might accrue to the timid individual, the question would have to be answered: Could I will that this act be universalized? In short, could I will that less than fully informed consent be a generalized practice? If I could not, then I would have to resist the urge to withhold information of possible risks for the potential student.

One could take a nonconsequentialist approach to this problem on grounds not necessarily Kantian in nature. For instance, it could be argued that the principle of personal autonomy is not one which should be set aside just because very good results would be obtained. It is arguable that by not informing the student fully, I restrict his liberty and that restrictions of liberty without legal due process are just not a morally acceptable practice. Thus, an act-based approach could be maintained on non-Kantian grounds.

While the most obvious problem of informed consent in experiential education lies in the realm of possibly hazardous activities, there are other areas that are equally, although not as obviously, troubling.

Suppose a young woman from an urban setting has signed up for a wilderness-based experiential education program. She has been informed about possible hazards and has signed statements indicating her understanding of these hazards. She has also been informed that if she quits the program for non-medical reasons, she will lose most of her tuition money.

She arrives for the course and discovers to her dismay that she will not be allowed to use any toilet paper for a month. She cannot drink coffee or tea because the program has declared these bad for her health. She is told to surrender her wristwatch to the authorities. She is from a very conservative background and discovers that she will be required to sleep under tarps with male students. She objects to all of these requirements and says that they are unreasonable and she wants to leave the course. However, she is told that if she leaves she will lose her tuition, since she is leaving for non-medical reasons.

I raise these issues because they present problems of informed consent that are not necessarily under the heading of hazardous activities. These issues are tied in closely with the question of financial matters because of the complicating role of finances in informed consent problems. One could retort to the young woman that she is free to leave at any time if she objects to any or all of the practices outlined above. However, the ethical problem is whether she really is free to quit, given the financial loss she will suffer. Not only will she lose her tuition, she will also lose her travel money, her time taken off from work, and other expenses connected with her participation in the program. **Is it right to spring surprises, of a possibly unpleasant nature, on students to which the students have not consented prior to entering the educational program?**

Drawing from the argument from autonomy and liberty, it seems clear that one is always on ethically shaky ground whenever one imposes unpleasant practices upon students who were not informed beforehand that they would have unpleasant surprises imposed upon them.

There are several ways the ethically concerned practitioner could go here. One possibility would be to make it possible for a student to leave a program at any time with a guarantee of complete financial reimbursement for all expenses incurred by the student, not only for medical reasons but also for informed consent reasons. This alternative presupposes lack of informed consent and is a post-facto solution to the problem. It reasons that not giving information is ethically right when a way out is provided. This solution seems unworkable, mainly for logistical reasons. Imagine having to plan a program and not knowing how many students will have to be reimbursed because of lack of informed consent. This solution is not only logistically problematic, it is also ethically problematic because it reasons that violations of autonomy and liberty are right if financial matters are handled to the advantage of the student. Imagine being told by your neighbor that she is going to steal your car for a week but that she will pay you for it later!

Another solution would be to detail every possible practice that could conceivably be unpleasant to every student and have all students sign releases of having been informed about these practices. This would guarantee personal autonomy while allowing programs to use unpleasant practices for educational benefit. At first glance, this alternative appears appealing. It provides the best of both values. However, it is possibly unworkable. It seems like an impossible task to predict, before the fact, what every student will find unpleasant. It would be as difficult to detail every unpleasant practice as it would be to detail every hazard, given the variability of those practices that are unpleasant and the variability of subjective responses to various practices.

A third possibility would be to have students sign a very broad statement that would inform them that certain programmatic practices will be used which deviate drastically from culturally accepted practices and which may be unpleasant. This option has the strength of at least warning the students that unusual and potentially unpleasant experiences will happen. At the same time, it would allow the programs to be flexible and able to function in a logistically practical manner.

As far as the financial aspects of this area of informed consent are concerned, I think a possible solution lies in what I call the "commensurability proportion." The commensurability proportion is an attempt to resolve the conflict between a program's need to plan financially and a student's need to be informed about what he is getting himself into. Put succinctly, the proportion allows for varying degrees of moral weight between programs and students. The more I have been informed about the practices I am getting myself into, the less claim I have to financial reimbursement. Proportionally, the less the program has informed me about what its actual practices are, the greater its responsibility to financially reimburse me when conflicts arise about informed consent.

My hunch is that most experiential education programs have dealt more with the issue of informed consent in terms of hazardous activities than they have non-hazardous aspects of programming. However, both aspects of informed consent go to the heart of what is meant by human autonomy and liberty. Therefore, it is vital for practitioners who are concerned about ethical issues to look carefully into the whole area of informed consent, whether about hazardous activities or other activities.

Endnotes / Chapter 3

1. M.D. Kirby, "Informed Consent: What Does It Mean?" The Journal of Medical Ethics 9. (1983),69.

2. Tom L. Beauchamp and LeRoy Walters, Contemporary Issues in Bioethics (Belmont, Dickenson Publishing Company, 1978), 134.

Chapter Three / Informed Consent

3. Beauchamp and Walters, 135.

4. John Dewey, <u>Logic</u> (New York: Irvington Publishers, 1982), 9, 10.

5. Tom Beauchamp and J. F. Childress <u>Principles of Biomedical Ethics</u> (New York: Oxford University Press,1979), 56, 57.

Chapter Four

Deception

The directors of a church youth conference had a goal of teaching the young people about the dangers and realities of state controlled, totalitarian interferences in religious freedom. The directors were agreed that an experiential approach to this problem would be a more effective teaching technique than simply giving a lecture on the issue. The conference was being held in a camp setting, removed from much contact with the outside world. Several adult church workers, not known to any of the young people, arrived on the scene. After supper, while the campers were cleaning up the dishes, the adult workers burst into the kitchen. They had stockings over their heads and they carried unloaded rifles and pistols. All of the young people were herded into a group and were informed that they were hostages and that the only way to secure their release was to sign a document renouncing their religious beliefs. Several campers began to cry. The cries were met with barked orders to shut up, else they would be shot. This scene went on for several hours, complete with interrogations, agreements to sign the documents, and some defiance of the orders. After a while the adults took off their masks, revealed their true identities, and began a group debriefing and counseling session with the young people. The conference leaders were pleased with their educational techniques. Several campers required professional counseling after leaving the conference. Several parents filed law suits against the conference leaders claiming psychological cruelty.

A group of students on a wilderness-based experiential education course were having a hard time learning the fundamentals of emergency first aid. They were not taking the lessons seriously and wanted to go climbing instead, claiming that first aid was not very important or difficult to learn. The instructor of the group had the assistant instructor sneak into the woods where she feigned a severe accident. Cosmetic devices were used to give the injury the look of an actual accident. Hearing her screams, the students ran over and were confronted by a scene of trauma that shocked many group members and impelled them into taking action. Several minutes later the students realized that the accident was staged. The instructors debriefed the group on the importance of first aid and several group members expressed their appreciation of the feigned accident. One member of the group was extremely angry that she had been deceived by the instructors.

These two examples, from very different types of experiential approaches to education, point out an ethical issue in experiential education that deserves some attention by practitioners. I am referring to the use of deception as an educational tool in order to attain certain educational goals. To deceive a person or group of people means to mislead that person or group into believing that something is true that is, in fact, not true. Ethicist Sissela Bok has referred to deception:

When we undertake to deceive others intentionally, we communicate messages meant to mislead them, meant to make them believe what we ourselves do not believe. We can do so through gesture, through disguise, by means of action or inaction, even through silence. [1]

Bok goes on to make a conceptual distinction between deception and lying. She writes:

Which of these innumerable deceptive messages are also lies? I shall define as a lie any intentionally deceptive message which is **stated.** *Such statements are most often made verbally or in writing, but can of course also be conveyed via smoke signals, Morse code, sign language, and the like. Deception, then, is the larger category, and lying forms part of it.* [2]

While Bok's characterization of deception as a broader notion than lying is theoretically interesting, for purposes of this book I refer to deception as inclusive of the narrower conception of lying. For instance, in the two examples just illustrated, both represent cases of deception. According to Bok's definition no lie was told, but people were deceived. My concern is with the broader issue of deception and not just with the narrower conception of lying.

There are two types of deception to be considered that help shed some light on the difficulties of this issue. It is useful to characterize acts of deception in terms of the ends to which the deceptive acts aim. I call these two types of deception **malevolent deception** and **benevolent deception.**

Malevolent deception is an act of deception that has as its end something that the deceived person would not find desirable or favorable to her own interests. For instance, suppose I wish to steal your stereo. In order to gain entrance to your house, I tell you about a sale at a store nearby so that you will leave your home. However, I know that all the goods on sale have already been sold. You leave. I enter your house and steal your stereo. You return, find your stereo stolen, and thank me for directing you to the store, even though all the goods were already sold. You then deal with the stolen stereo, having no idea that I am the one who stole your stereo. My act of deception here can be characterized as an act of malevolent deception. I did the deceiving in order to obtain an end that was against your interests.

Most acts of malevolent deception are not particularly interesting to examine here because, as in the above example, the deception seems so clearly wrong. However, some acts of malevolent deception could possibly be construed as ethically right. Recall my example from Chapter 1 about the drunken wife beater asking where his wife is. Suppose I deceive him about where she is. Clearly it is his expressed interest to find her. In a sense, my act of deception violates his interests and could, therefore, be called malevolent. However, I could reply that I did not deceive him in order to **hurt** him, but rather to **protect** him from doing something that will work against his interests once he is sober again. Therefore, I could argue that I acted benevolently and not malevolently. A better example of a morally acceptable malevolently deceptive act might be something like this. As I write these words, Ted Bundy, the infamous serial killer, has just been executed in Florida. Suppose the only way I had to catch this killer and stop his killing was to deceive him. Here, unlike the drunken wife beater, I am not deceiving Bundy for Bundy's protection. I am deceiving him in order to destroy him, either through permanent incarceration or through execution (whether or not capital punishment is morally right is an issue I cannot take the time to address here). An argument could be made that my act of malevolent deception to Bundy was right because by getting rid of him I have given him his due for his evil acts. In other words, a case could be made that malevolent acts are the only proper acts to make to someone like Bundy.

A benevolent act of deception is one in which the act is done in order to attain an end that the person being deceived finds desirable and in her best interests. Drawing from the two examples at the opening of this chapter, an argument can be made that both the church and the wilderness leaders were acting deceptively only in order to help achieve laudable educational ends. Benevolent acts of deception in experiential education range from blatant acts of deception (like the first aid example) to more subtle acts of deception. I can recall several instances with students in the field where I deliberately put a student on a rock climb that I knew beforehand she could not complete. Usually these were the super achiever students who had not met a single challenge on the course that they did not complete successfully and with aplomb. I would suggest that she attempt a **difficult** climb (notice that I did **not** say **impossible**) in order to push her limits. In a sense this was an act of deception because I did not previously characterize the climb as impossible. This is a much more subtle act of deception than my opening examples. Nevertheless, it is still deception.

It is probably safe to say that the acts of deception that occur within contexts of most experiential education programs are acts of benevolent deception and not acts of malevolent deception. Therefore, I want to spend most of my time here on the morality of benevolent acts of deception. **Is it right to deceive our students in order to obtain good educational aims?**

One way to go here is to tie in the issue of deception immediately with the issue of informed consent. It can be argued that deceptive practices are ethically right when the students know before the fact that they will be deceived. I recently conducted a training session for instructors working on the Mankato State University High Ropes Course. I told them before we began the training session that I was going to fake various emergency situations in order to test their reactions and competency in emergencies. In a sense, I told them the rules of the game before the game started and then used deception within those rules. Thus, it could be argued that deception, when conducted within the context of rules **previously agreed to**, is ethically right.

The move to place deception within the scope of informed consent and rule governed practices is useful but it is also troubling. It is troubling because an argument can be made that once someone has been told that she will be deceived upon occasion, it is not really deception anymore. In other words, what started out as a discussion of deception wound up as a discussion about the rules of the game which allowed for deception. Imagine, for instance, that you are playing a game of football. The quarterback drops back, fakes a pass, fakes a handoff, and then runs the ball. Have you really been deceived by that quarterback? According to the strict definition supplied by Sissela Bok, you have been. Would you, therefore, hold the quarterback morally blameworthy? One can hardly blame a quarterback for playing a game that has a rule which permits deception. In fact, the game **demands** that the quarterback use deception effectively in order to be a good quarterback.

The reason I find this move troubling is that it is too easy an out. What started out as an ethical issue converted into a discussion of the rules of the game. A possibly immoral act (deception) becomes moral if the rules allow for such acts of deception and it is immoral if the deception is not previously agreed to as an acceptable practice.

But are all acts of deception not previously agreed to unethical? Take the deceptive use of the simulated first aid accident. Suppose those students had not been told prior to attending the course that deceptive practices were part of the course. Would the instructor's desire that the students be protected by their enhanced appreciation for first aid make the deceptive act morally right?

A consequentialist approach to ethics would have little trouble with the deceptive use of the simulated accident **if it resulted in good consequences for the students.** Benevolent deception becomes morally justified if good results accrue to the person or persons being deceived. Drawing from a utilitarian calculation of the act's moral worth, one might well conclude that the enhanced knowledge of first aid and the concomitant happiness that was achieved by the students rendered the deceptive act a good act.

The nonconsequentialist approach to the first aid situation is going to focus in on the act of deception itself. Drawing from Kant, the hard question must be faced by those two instructors: **Would they will that deception be a universalized technique in education?** If the answer is no, then such acts of deception must be stopped from a Kantian perspective.

The whole issue of benevolent deception in experiential education becomes even more complicated by a further distinction which must be made. Recall my definition of benevolent deception earlier in this chapter: A benevolent act of deception is one in which the act is done only in order to attain an end that the person being deceived finds desirable and in her best interests. The word interest here is very important. Prima facie, it seems obvious what my own best interests are. They are what I define them to be. But what if what I think is in my best interests is not in fact in my best interest? The distinction must be made between interests, wants, and needs.

Suppose I say that what I want is what is in my best interest. What I want is to drive my automobile at high speeds after I have become legally drunk. Is it really in my best interest to pursue what I want? In this case, it seems clear that what I want is not in my best interest. In the case of the simulated first aid incident, what the students wanted was not to waste time on first aid lessons. But, clearly it was in their best interest to deny their wants and to have them learn first aid.

What I need is not necessarily the same thing as what I want. What I need is also not necessarily dependent upon my acknowledgment that I need it. For instance, I may really want to eat a high cholesterol, high fat diet. I, therefore, eat this diet. I have my blood cholesterol checked and discover that it is extremely high. What I needed was to alter my diet even though I did not acknowledge that it needed changing.

The point here is that a benevolent act of deception is defined in terms of the best interests of the student. However, the notion of best interests is itself a very complicated affair at best. Indeed, it is possible that the best interests of someone can only be achieved through deceiving that person when that person does not know her best interests. It is this formulation of the benevolent

Chapter Four / Deception

deception argument that is most often put forth by those who use the practice in their professional activities. As thus stated, the argument for the use of benevolent deception in experiential education seems fairly strong.

Although a Kantian argument can be used against deceptive practices, there are other ones that can be mustered to attack the use of deception as an educational tool. One of the strongest is rooted in the very nature of the student-teacher relationship itself.

Fundamental to the teacher-student relationship is the quest for knowledge. Presumably, the teacher knows and the student does not know. The whole point of the establishment of this relationship is to move from ignorance to knowledge. Anything that interferes with the quest for knowledge can be called an impediment to education. Imagine entering into a relationship with a teacher as her pupil and not knowing whether that teacher really knows what she says she knows. In other words, she may claim to know, but in fact she does not know. Therefore, there would be no reason to trust that person's ability to teach. Trust is the key term here. **It can be argued that unless students trust their teachers, the whole task of moving from ignorance to knowledge is doomed from the start.** For if I cannot trust my teacher's claim to know, then there is no reason to pursue the relationship further. Once the bond of trust between student and teacher has been violated, the goal of the pursuit of knowledge becomes problematic at best.

If I am your teacher and I deceive you, why then should you trust that I will not continue to deceive you in the future? Once I have led you down the path of deception without your consent, then it is at least possible that I may continue to deceive you. The bond of trust between student and teacher is one which is easily broken. Once broken, it is possible that it is not easily restored:

The veneer of social trust is often thin. As lies spread - by imitation, or in retaliation, or to forestall suspected deception - trust is damaged. Yet trust is a social good to be protected just as much as the air we breathe or the water we drink. When it is damaged, the community as a whole suffers; and when it is destroyed, societies falter and collapse. [3]

Granted, the students in the first aid simulation have learned a valuable lesson about the subject matter at hand. That is not at issue here. However, another lesson has been learned by those students—that their teacher will deceive them in order to pursue the goal of learning the lesson at hand.

Another argument that can be brought to bear against the use of benevolent deceptions in experiential education is to refer, again, to the principle of the liberty and autonomy of individuals. When I deceive you, I am limiting your liberty and your autonomy. Your liberty is limited because the act of deception puts you in a position of acting towards what you think is reality when it is not reality. If you had known what reality really was, you might have chosen differently than you did. Your autonomy is also violated because I have chosen to obtain certain responses from you that you might not have wanted to give. As Thomas Hill has written:

But now it emerges that ideals of autonomy not only oppose undiscoverable benevolent lies; they also oppose lies which risk discovery of a breach of trust for discovery of such lies encourages us to be distrustful and suspicious and so less able to make use of even honest answers trustworthy persons give us; and this limits our opportunities for rational control over our lives. These conclusions, of course, are both hypothetical and intuitive: that is, the argument has been that if one accepts certain principles of autonomy, then one has reasons to refrain from benevolent lies. [4]

How, then, should ethically concerned experiential education practitioners proceed with this issue? Clearly, a strong case can be made for the careful use of benevolent deception. Equally strong arguments can be mustered to counter the use of deception. Once again, Sissela Bok offers useful guidance. She offers two criteria to test whether an act of deception is right. The first is that we be willing to make our use of deception publicly known:

Moral justification, therefore, cannot be exclusive or hidden; it has to be capable of being made public. In going beyond the purely private, it attempts to transcend also what is merely subjective. [5]

In the case of the church group and the capture of the young people, the public outcry about the deceptive practices has been loud and angry. However, my experience with examples like the first aid simulation has been that, while controversial, the responses have not been nearly so loud nor angry. However, some students have protested loudly and angrily, even to fairly benign uses of deception. These voices should be listened to.

The second criteria proposed by Bok is for those using deception to ask themselves if they would object to this act if it were done to them:

It requires us to seek concrete and open performance of an exercise crucial to ethics the Golden Rule, basic to so many religious and moral traditions. We must share the perspective of those affected by our choices, and ask how we would react if the lies we are contemplating were told to us. [6]

It should be clear that the use of deception in experiential education is, at best, a controversial and ethically problematic practice. I think one of the most important distinctions to bear in mind, as a practical matter, is the difference between deception as an aspect of informed consent and deception that has not been consented to. I might well not blame the deceptive quarterback, while I might find arguments to condemn the deceptive church leaders.

Some interesting perspectives on deception as a violation of individual

Chapter Four / Deception

liberty and autonomy are contained in the chapter of this book on "Paternalism." Most uses of benevolent deception by experiential educators are done by practitioners motivated by paternalistic concern for their students. Whether or not paternalistic interventions in students' lives through deception are morally justified is quite problematic.

Endnotes / Chapter 4

1. Sissela Bok, Lying: Moral Choice in Public and Private Life (New York: Vintage Books, 1979), 14.

2. Bok, Lying, 14.

3. Bok, Lying, 28.

4. Thomas E. Hill, Jr. "Autonomy and Benevolent Lies," The Journal of Value Inquiry 18 (1984), 265.

5. Bok, 97.

6. Bok, 98.

Chapter Five

Secrecy

A group of students on a wilderness-based experiential education program are planning their final expedition route. The topographic maps are laid out and the group has settled on a tentative route. Before going on the expedition the students must have the route approved by their instructors. The head instructor studies the proposed route and notices that the students will end up bushwacking through a mosquito-infested swamp for a significant period of time. The instructor refrains from mentioning this fact and approves the route. Upon the completion of the expedition, the students angrily confront the instructor and demand why he did not inform them of the swamp. The instructor replies that his withholding of the information was done only in order that the students encounter a consequence of their route finding, and that had he told them what he knew, they probably would have missed a valuable learning experience.

An instructor has a particularly troublesome group of juvenile delinquents. The group is not working well together and there is a high degree of intra-group hostility. One of the students approaches the instructor and asks if he can speak confidentially. The instructor agrees to the request and the student then informs the instructor that the reason the group is fighting so much is because one of the students has a bottle full of Librium pills and he is giving out small quantities to his friends. Therefore, the group is in conflict over who gets how many pills. The instructor is unsure how to proceed with his newfound information, secretly given.

The issue of secrecy in experiential education is closely related to the issue of deception but it is not the same thing. Where a deceptive act is one deliberately designed to induce people into believing that what is false is true, the secretive act is simply the withholding of information and not the distortion of information. Deception is active by nature and secrecy is passive by nature.

The whole issue of secrecy is complicated by the different ways in which

Chapter Five / Secrecy

secrecy manifests itself as an ethical problem for practitioners. For instance, in the opening example of this chapter, the issue was the use of secrecy as an educational tool for the goal of having students come to know what they did not know before. The second example concerned the issue of having assured a student that the teacher would keep their conversation secret and confidential. Another way in which the secrecy issue manifests itself in experiential education includes the withholding of information learned about a student while on a course. This information could be withheld from any number of information seekers including family, friends, employers, therapists and other educators who will have future contact with that student. For instance, suppose I have a student on a course who intends to become an airline pilot upon his completion of the course. I learn from first-hand experience that he handles himself very poorly while under stress, and I make the judgment that he shows signs of a behavior pattern that would make him a dangerous pilot. Ought I to keep this information secret if I am asked to write a job reference for that student? In other words, should students of experiential education practitioners have a claim to secrecy, much as a patient has with a physician or a penitent has with a priest?

The opening example of the withholding of information from students is one which is ubiquitous in education in general. It becomes particularly acute for experiential educators. One of the determining characteristics of experiential education is its concern with the process of learning as well as with the content of learning. Education which is exclusively concerned with information assimilation will find that the rapid elimination of ignorance through quick presentations of information suffices for learning. For the traditional educator, learning is a fairly simple affair and the presence of ignorance is not to be tolerated. It is to be eliminated as rapidly as possible through the teacher's superior quantity of information.

The experiential educator oftentimes embraces ignorance on the part of students. Indeed, it is commonplace to find experiential educators working with students' ignorance as a strong ally in the process of learning. One of the classic examples of this comes from one of the earliest experiential educators, Socrates. In the dialogue, Meno, Plato describes an interaction between the teacher (Socrates) and a young slave boy. Socrates is attempting to teach geometry to the ignorant slave boy. As Socrates works with the slave boy, he describes the process with a young man named Meno:

*Socrates: Observe, Meno, the stage he has reached on the path of recollection. At the beginning he did not know the side of the square of eight feet. Nor indeed does he know it now, but then he thought he knew it and answered boldly, as was appropriate - **he left no perplexity**. Now, however, he does feel* *perplexed. Not only does he not know the answer; he doesn't even think he knows.*

Meno: Quite true

Socrates: Isn't he in a better position now in relation to what he didn't know?

Meno: I admit that too.

Socrates: So in perplexing him and numbing him like the sting ray, have we done him any harm?

Meno: I think not.

-and later-

Socrates: **Do you suppose then that he would have attempted to look for, or learn what he thought he knew, though he did not, before he was thrown into perplexity, became aware of his ignorance, and felt a desire to know?**

Meno: No

Socrates: Then the numbing process was good for him?

Meno: I agree. [1]

Notice that Socrates does not confront the slave boy's ignorance with a rapid-fire lecture designed to eliminate the boy's ignorance as quickly as possible. Rather, Socrates, in a sense, holds his own knowledge as a secret and attempts to impel the boy into perplexity before going on to learn the geometry. Socrates refers to the attempt to impel one into realization of one's own ignorance as "the numbing process." **Whenever we impel a student into perplexity rather than simply informing him, we are keeping our knowledge secret from him until he is ready for that knowledge.** This is the heart of the issue.

I'll never forget an incident that happened during the summer of 1975. I was instructing for Pacific Crest Outward Bound School in the Cascade Mountains of Oregon. My assistant and I had a particularly able, but arrogant, group of students. Two or three students had taken control of the navigation tasks from the group, with the group's permission. I noticed one afternoon that the compass bearing they had taken was 180 degrees off what it should have been. They had simply placed the compass improperly down on the map. In their haste, they took off on the wrong bearing. My assistant asked me if I was going to inform them about their mistake. I said no. Instead, we followed them all afternoon on the wrong bearing. They became quite lost ("numbed") and were in total confusion about why they were lost ("perplexity"). When we told them what they had done wrong, several students became quite angry and said that I should not have kept my knowledge of their mistake secret.

An argument can be made that the core of experiential education, as opposed to traditional education, is in the key role of impelling students into perplexity **prior** to providing much new information. Logically speaking, it

Chapter Five / Secrecy

could be said that perplexity is a necessary condition for the experiential approach to happen at all, regardless of physical setting. If genuine impelling into perplexity is morally wrong, then that immorality is a serious threat to the overall mission of experiential education practitioners.

It seems true that any genuine impelling into perplexity demands that the practitioner hold at least some of his knowledge secret, at least for a while. It is also very important not to confuse a student's resistance to realizing his own ignorance (manifested by anger very often) with being morally wrong. Merely becoming angry does not necessarily satisfy that which has made me angry is, therefore, immoral. That which has made me angry may be immoral, but it is not necessarily immoral. Later in the <u>Meno</u>, Socrates is confronted by a man called Anytus, who becomes angry when Socrate's arguments, which render Anytus' certitude about issues less than certain, begin to perplex Anytus.

Anytus: You seem to me, Socrates, to be too ready to run people down. My advice to you, if you will listen to it, is to be careful. I dare say that in all cities it is easier to do a man harm than good, and it is certainly so here, as I expect you know yourself.

Socrates: Anytus seems angry, Meno, and I am not surprised. [2]

Anytus confuses Socrates' impelling students into perplexity with being "too ready to run people down." It is worth noting here that Socrates was condemned to death by the people of Athens. One of Socrates' chief accusers at the trial was Anytus. At his trial Socrates replies to Anytus' charges by saying;

Suppose, then, that you acquit me, and pay no attention to Anytus, who has said that either I should not have appeared before this court at all, or, since I have appeared here, I must be put to death, because if I once escaped your sons would all immediately become utterly demoralized by putting the teaching of Socrates into practice. Suppose that, in view of this, you said to me, Socrates, on this occasion we shall disregard Anytus and acquit you, but only on one condition, that you give up spending your time on this quest and stop philosophizing. If we catch you going on in the same way, you shall be put to death.

-and later-

Well, supposing, as I said, that you should offer to acquit me on these terms, I should reply, Gentlemen ... I owe a greater obedience to God than to you, and ... I shall never stop practicing philosophy and exhorting you and elucidating the truth for everyone that I meet. [3]

Socrates' point is that he has no alternative as a teacher than to do as he has done. The teacherly role in assisting students in their pursuit of truth precludes him from changing his behavior.

The reply of the experiential educator to an angry student must be rooted in the nature of the student-teacher relationship. Whereas **deception** of a student can result in the loss of trust and other negative results (outlined in the "Deception" chapter), the keeping of a secret is a different matter. **In the case of secrecy, it is the student who is already deceived and not the teacher who is doing the deceiving.** The withholding of information is merely a teaching tool designed to remove the state of ignorance in which the student exsists.

Students may get angry. Socrates was sentenced to death for his refusal to stop teaching. That people may get angry is a psychological issue and not necessarily a moral issue for the practitioner. Indeed, following Socrates' lead, the practitioner could argue that it is immoral **not** to impel people into perplexity. For without perplexity, education may, possibly, not ever take place at all.

The motive behind the keeping of a secret seems vital here. The experiential education practitioner uses secrecy in order to achieve a good end and not in order to achieve an evil end. As with the deception issue, the distinction should be made between benevolent secrets and malevolent secrets. Educationally speaking, it can be argued that a benevolent secret is one which is kept only in order to enhance the learning of the student or students.

Unfortunately, I have seen a few examples of experiential education practitioners withholding information in order to gain the psychological upper hand over their students. The old saying that "knowledge is power" has some truth to it. It seems clear that such uses of secrecy on the part of practitioners can be dismissed as immoral rather easily. This is because the secret is held, not in order to make teaching more effective, but in order to raise the low self-esteem of the practitioner.

It should also be kept in mind that the keeping of a secret can rather easily become an act of deception. For instance, students might specifically ask an instructor if a given route is a good one. If the instructor knows it is a bad one and replies yes, then the issue is deception and not secrecy. In short, lying about the fact that you are holding a secret is very different from holding a secret. The lie is an act of deception and not merely withholding of information.

Once again, informed consent can be useful for the discussion of secrecy. It is a rather simple matter to inform students before the fact that secrets may be kept in order to facilitate learning. If experiential education really is fundamentally different from traditional information assimilation education, and if one of these differences lies in the Socratic technique of impelling students into real perplexity, why not simply inform students what these differences are before they begin the experiential process. The whole psychological issue of anger may rest squarely in the informed consent aspect of secrecy. Students could be expecting traditional, quick information assimilation-type education, and the anger could be the result of expectations not having been met.

The second example from the opening of this chapter illustrates another set of problems of secrecy pertinent to experiential education practitioners. Recall that the student confided in the instructor about the illicit drug use only on condition that the instructor would keep the conversation secret. This raises the broader ethical issue of the use and misuse of secrecy within the context of the student-teacher relationship that does not involve specific issues of learning methodology as just discussed above. As presented in the opening example, the issue of secrecy is intimately tied in with the making of a promise. Put succinctly, the issue is about my promising to keep a student's confidence secret.

There is little ethical conflict if my promise to keep a secret does not involve any harm to others. For instance, a student confides in me about his conflicts with his parents. I listen, serve a counseling role, and keep my promise of secrecy. This example of secrecy presents little of moral interest. There is not a conflict of value here with which to wrestle. We keep the promise of secrecy because to violate the secret pact would be to deceive the student, with all of the attendant problems inherent in deception.

The issue of secrecy and a promise to keep secrets becomes ethically interesting when my promise to keep a secret involves possible or probable harm to others. This issue has received a great deal of attention in the medical, psychological, and pastoral counseling professions. The famous Hippocratic Oath, a cornerstone of medical ethics, has the following paragraph in it:

What I may see or hear in the course of the treatment or even outside of treatment in regard to the life of men, which on no account one must spread abroad, I will keep to myself holding such things shameful to be spoken about.[4]

But what if, during a course of treatment, a physician discovers that a patient has an incurable disease that is also communicable to others. Furthermore, the patient also confides in the physician that no attempt will be made to stop the spread of this disease to others. This is precisely what the medical ethicists are dealing with in the AIDS issue. Should that physician keep the promise made to the patient concerning secrecy?

The conflict involves the competing claims of the public good versus the private secret. This is precisely the issue lurking in the shadows of the second opening example of this chapter.

One way of approaching this issue is to make a distinction between making promises of secrecy that can be kept and making promises of secrecy that cannot be kept. In other words, there is a difference between making a promise that I know beforehand that I can keep and making a promise that I know I will not keep. One of the classic examples of this issue is illustrated by Immanuel Kant when he discusses the case of the man who desperately needs to borrow money but knows that he will never be able to repay it. Unless the man promises to repay the loan, he will not receive it. In his application of the categorical imperative to this case, Kant writes:

For the universality of a law which says that anyone who believes himself to be in need could promise what he pleased with the intention of not fulfilling it would make the promise itself and the end to be accomplished by it impossible; no one would believe what was promised to him but would only laugh at any such assertion as vain pretense. [5]

Kant's message is that if we make promises that we have no intention of keeping, we evade the very function of a promise in the first place. Therefore, it is imperative that we not make promises we do not intend to keep. This line of reasoning would include promises to keep secrets like the one made to the experiential education student about the drug use. This is a clear application of the nonconsequentialist's ethical methodology to the issue at hand.

For the consequentialist, especially an act utilitarian, the case of the pledge to secrecy to the drug-using student would have to be evaluated in terms of the broader social good and not just in terms of the act of the pledge to secrecy. As a consequentialist, acting under the guidance of act utilitarianism, one might very well argue that the only ethically right thing to do in the drug case would be to protect the broader good by using the secretly supplied information to protect the group from harm.

One way to go with this that might be of practical use to practitioners would be to follow Kant's lead and not make promises that one knows one cannot keep. For instance, when asked by the student for a pledge to secrecy, the instructor has an alternative to a simple yes or no. Instead, he could tell that student that he will honor the secret **only if it will not harm others**. This would be to invoke the principle of informed consent once again. Before I made the promise to the student, I could outline to him that my pledge to secrecy has certain conditions attached to it and here is what those conditions are. The student could then make the decision whether or not to proceed with his disclosures. This approach would serve to use the Kantian criteria while at the same time using the utilitarian criteria. No deception will have occurred since the student was informed **before the fact** that his secret would not be kept if it would result in harm to others or even to himself.

Finally, the issue of secrecy as it relates to those affected by the secret outside the confines of the immediate educational setting must be addressed. Recall the example of the student who wants to be an airline pilot. Ought the instructor to share his insights about that student's behavior under pressure in the requested reference? One way to go would be to simply lie on the reference. This alternative seems patently wrong on grounds so obvious as not to warrant discussion here.

Chapter Five / Secrecy

Another alternative would be to not lie but, instead, simply not mention this aspect of the student's behavior. This would be to keep the insights secret and not to deliberately lie.

The third alternative would be to tell the truth, not keep any secrets, and thereby hurt the student's chances of obtaining the pilot job. In the "Deception" chapter I used the example of the football quarterback who practiced deception because the rules of the game demanded that he effectively use deception as part of the game. One could reason here that once the student asked for a reference from the instructor, that student was thereby choosing to play the rule-governed game of reference writing and that these rules demand that the reference writer be truthful and not keep relevant information secret. Thus, in a sense, the student gave his permission **implicitly** by asking for the reference in the first place.

An example from medical ethics is useful here. Ordinarily a physician is pledged to keep his patient's medical information secret. However, what about the case where the reason the patient is in the clinic in the first place is in order to receive a medical examination to determine if he is fit for some future activity, say, employment. The physician finds out that the person is not fit. Should that information be kept secret? Of course not, because the patient voluntarily submitted to the examination in order that his condition not be kept secret. Again, this is an example of rule-governed behavior. Similar reasoning could be applied to the reference writing example.

The issue gets complicated when the information that the instructor has obtained does not fall under the rubric of rule-governed sharing of information. Is there an implied or explicit obligation on the part of educators to keep secret, information obtained about a student while under the tutelage of a teacher? In other words, should students expect the same sort of confidentiality from their teachers that they expect from their physicians and priests?

A very strong argument can be made that the student-teacher relationship is at least as intimate and time honored as the physician-patient relationship or the priest-penitent relationship. There is a very powerful section of Plato's dialogue, **Theaetetus,** where Socrates makes a direct comparison between the student-teacher relationship and the physician-patient relationship. Socrates refers to the relationship between a woman in childbirth and her midwife as an example of this point.

Socrates: My art of midwifery is in general like theirs; the only difference is that my patients are men, not women, and my concern is not with the body but with the soul that is in travail of birth. And the highest point of my art is the power to prove by every test whether the offspring of a young man's thought is a false phantom or instinct with life and truth.

-and later-

In yet another way those who seek my company have the same experience as a woman with child; they suffer the pains of labor and, by night and day, are full of distress far greater than a woman's, and my art has power to bring on these pangs or to alloy them. [6]

(Readers should remember that this was written twenty-three hundred years ago, and treat the sexist allusion of students as males with that fact in mind.)

If Socrates is right that the teacher's art is similar to the midwife's art, then it seems reasonable that experiential education students should expect a similar level of confidentiality and secrecy from their teachers and instructors that they would from their health practitioners. There could at least exist a prima facie claim to similar treatment. Again, I am not referring to rule-governed practices like references, grades on transcripts and the like. Rather, the claim is made as a **general** statement of the teacher-student relationship as such.

Endnotes / Chapter 5

1. Plato, <u>Meno</u>, in <u>Plato: The Collected Dialogues,</u> ed. Edith Hamilton and Huntington Cairns (Princeton: Princeton University Press, 1961), 368.

2. Plato, <u>Meno</u>, 379.

3. Plato, <u>Apology</u>, 15 (Princeton Edition)

4. "The Hippocratic Oath" Quoted in <u>Contemporary Issues in Bioethics</u>, ed. Tom L. Beauchamp and Leroy Walters (Belmont: Wadsworth Publishing, 1979), 138.

5. Immanuel Kant, <u>Foundations of the Metaphysics of Morals</u> (Indianapolis: Bobbs Merrill, 1959), 40.

6. Plato, <u>Theaetetus</u>, 855, 856 (Princeton Edition)

Chapter Six

Captive Populations

Ernie was a 14-year-old inner city boy who had been in chronic trouble with the local juvenile court. His court record included breaking and entering, car theft, truancy, and illegal use of drugs. He had been treated, unsuccessfully, with talk therapy, incarceration in the juvenile detention center, and a work release program. His social worker decided that a new wilderness-based experiential education program might be just the thing for Ernie. She told Ernie and his parents about the program and convinced them that the wilderness program was worth a try. Ernie entered the program and 16 days into the course was doing the rock climbing phase of the program. He had attempted several climbs and had given up trying to do each climb every time he hit a difficult move. On each occasion he insisted on being lowered to the ground. The instructor complied with Ernie's wishes. Finally, the instructor decided that Ernie would benefit from finishing at least one climb. Near the top of one climb, Ernie hit a difficult move and asked to be lowered. The instructor replied that, on this climb, being lowered was not an option and that Ernie must complete the climb or at least try harder. Ernie protested this reply from the instructor and demanded that he be lowered immediately. The instructor told the belayer to hold the rope tight, so that Ernie could not climb down. Ernie then threatened to untie his waist loop, thereby going off belay. The instructor told the belayer to tighten the rope even tighter, so that the belay knot could not be untied. Finally, resigned to his fate, Ernie made one last attempt at the hard move. He made the move, finished the climb and cried for joy at the top of the climb. Ernie's success on the climb changed his whole attitude towards the program. He finished the program successfully and reported to his parents and social worker that being forced to finish that climb had made all the difference in his success. Ernie never again was arrested and never again came into contact with the juvenile court authorities.

The story of Ernie raises a set of ethical issues in experiential education which should be addressed here. It is becoming clear that experiential education, especially the adventure-based wing, is an effective form of treatment and education for various populations with legal, psychological, and other problems. Many of these people are sent on programs against their will or at least as a condition for obtaining some desired end. For instance, I have heard of psychologists and psychiatrists who give troubled adolescents the choice of participation in an experiential education program or being confined to a psychiatric hospital. In Ernie's case the choice was between the wilderness program or confinement in the juvenile detention center.

It is important to get clear that the issue at hand is not the psychological issue of the therapeutic effectiveness of various programs. Rather, the issue is about unique moral issues surrounding the use of experiential education techniques with students who are there against their will or who are there under some sort of coercion. **For definitional purposes, I shall refer to a captive population as any student or group of students who are in a given program because of being ordered or coerced into being there rather than through their own free initiative.** A juvenile delinquent under the power of the court's officers (judges, social workers) fits this definition nicely.

A useful starting point for discussing this issue is to go back to the whole issue of risk-benefit analysis. I argued in Chapter 2 that it is possible that a symmetry exists between the amount of benefit that may be gained by a student and the amount of risk that is ethically acceptable. If the student stands to gain a great deal from being exposed to risk, then it is arguable that that risk is more acceptable. If there is little to be gained by the risky activity, then justifying impelling students into the activity becomes more difficult.

Among the various student groups that practitioners encounter, it is possible, even probable, that the groups which stand to gain the most from experiential education programs are the captive populations. As more and more research reveals that experiential education is a viable option, educationally and psychologically for captive populations, the justification for using experiential techniques becomes stronger.

On purely utilitarian grounds, if it can be shown that juvenile delinquency recidivism rates drop from 80% to 40% as the direct result of participation in experiential education programs, the attendant risks of these programs may be ethically acceptable for these populations.

However, this argument comes to a screeching halt when confronted by the following issues. The core of the argument in the Informed Consent chapter was that it is vital that a participant be as fully informed about risks and benefits as possible prior to being impelled into potentially dangerous situations. Drawing from the principles of liberty and autonomy, it was argued that people could give their consent based upon having been well informed. The critical problem that comes up here is that captive populations are not operating from positions of autonomy and liberty in the first place. A person under the jurisdiction of a court of law is hardly a person who is autonomous and free. By definition, that person has lost his or her autonomy and his or her freedom. **How, then, can a person who is not autonomous or free possibly give truly informed consent?**

The informed part of informed consent is not a problem for the captive population groups. An argument can be made that a woman in jail can be as informed about risks and benefits as any other reasonable person. As far as simply being informed is concerned, this seems true.

The problem is not with becoming informed but is with the consent issue. If I have the choice between sitting in a jail or a detention center and attending an adventure-based experiential education program, how much actual consent am I really giving? It is arguable that there is very little consent being given and, therefore, the use of risk is questionable at best.

What emerges is an ethical dilemma that is among the more troublesome ethical dilemmas in experiential education. On the one hand are groups of students who, potentially, have the most to gain from experiential education programming. On the other hand, many of these groups are the least capable of giving their consent due to their status as captives.

One way of dealing with this is to acknowledge the fact that consent is artificial at best with captive populations and to refuse to use much dangerous programming with these groups and rely, instead, on perceived risk exclusively. However, as pointed out in the Risk/Benefit chapter, even so-called "perceived risk" has at least a modicum of actual risk built into it.

One of the presuppositions of the argument against risky activities with captive populations is that consent is not possible unless the person is autonomous and free. That may be true, but the concepts of autonomy and liberty must be clearly applied in terms of where they are restricted. It could be argued that the delinquent boy in a detention center is neither autonomous nor free, only in that he cannot leave the detention center. It could also be argued that any alternative that presents itself as an option to that which restricts autonomy and liberty **increases** the person's freedom. The person **could** elect to stay in detention and pass up the opportunity to attend the experiential education program. In this sense, informed consent could be given.

A key distinction arises that may be of practical help to practitioners. It seems clear that there is a difference between giving a student an **order** and giving

Chapter Six / Captive Populations

the student an **opportunity**. If I order someone to participate in an activity and that person is my captive, then that person can hardly be called a free agent. However, if I present my captive with an opportunity to do something and that person really has the option of not doing that activity, then that person can be called partially free. Recall that Ernie, in the opening example of this chapter, initially was given the opportunity to do the rock climb. As the activity progressed, Ernie became a captive, not only in the sense of being referred under court order, but he became even more of a captive because of the increasing dependence of his life on the belay rope the further he got off the ground. What started out as an activity that Ernie could give consent to (remember that he continually withdrew his consent by asking to be lowered to the ground) turned in a very few minutes into Ernie's becoming the instructor's captive. Ernie's life was dependent upon the belay rope and the instructor had control of this rope. Therefore, Ernie's life was dependent upon the instructor. In this sense Ernie was transformed from at least a partially free student to the complete captive of the instructor. This transformation from student to captive manifested itself as the shift was made from the student's **opportunity** to do the climb to the instructor's **order** that the student do the climb.

What emerges is an important distinction between students as **institutional** captives and students as **activity** captives. A student who is in an experiential education program against her will can be classified as an institutional captive. At the same time that institution could have within its operational processes, rules which provide some freedom to the participants to give their consent within that confining institution. For instance, a prisoner in a state maximum security prison has reached what might be the ultimate level of captivity. Nevertheless, within that environment, the prisoners can give or withdraw their consent to certain practices. An excellent example of this is in the use of prisoners for medical research. A great deal of attention has been given to this issue as far as informed consent is concerned. What has emerged from this debate is the notion that even prisoners in maximum security prisons must have the real option of not giving their consent to being experimented on. Thus, the prisoners are institutionally captive but free to give consent to specific activities. They are also free not to give consent to certain activities, and that freedom is institutionally protected.

Experiential education could draw from the example of medical research on prisoners. A way of operating ethically with captive populations might be to keep the distinction between institutional and activity-based captivity very clear. Just because a student may not be free to withdraw consent to being in the program in the first place, it does not follow that the student cannot give consent once she is within a given program.

Chapter Six / Captive Populations

There is more to the institutional consent issue than has been addressed so far in this chapter. I have suggested that a delinquent boy or girl in some sense may be free to consent or not consent to participating in an experiential education program in general. Ernie **could** have chosen to stay in detention. A real ethical danger lurks in this answer. **Whether or not a consent to participate in a given program is freely given must be evaluated in terms of the alternative consequences if that consent had not been given.** I have suggested that Ernie was free to stay in detention. Therefore, he was free to reject or accept participation in the experiential education program. However, suppose Ernie was being beaten and raped while in detention. In other words, suppose the consequences of not giving consent to participate in the experiential education program were so severe that Ernie really had little or no choice but to participate. It seems clear that it would be ethically disingenuous to say that Ernie was giving free consent, when, in fact, the alternative was rape and beatings. In short, the negative consequences of not giving consent could render what appeared initially to be a free act, really an act done under penalty of very bad consequences for the student. If this were the case, the student acted under coercion and was not really free at all to withhold consent.

A similar ethical danger lurks in terms of **positive** consequences that could come to a student if the consent is given. Suppose I am from a poverty background, I am having trouble in school, and there exists an opportunity for me to better myself by participating in a governmental program that will provide me with financial assistance and special educational programs. In order for me to be in this program, however, I must consent to participate in all activities presented by that program. These include certain high-risk activities. If I refuse to participate in a given activity, I will forfeit certain positive consequences. The presence of contingent positive benefits becomes, then, another form of coercion. If it is coercive, it limits freedom and if it limits freedom, it limits my ability to give consent. To say that a student could always leave the program in general as a consequence of not giving consent to a given activity, thereby forfeiting a number of positive consequences, is as ethically troublesome as the same reasoning applied to negative consequences.

Although the issue of the institutionally captive student is troublesome, it seems to be the case that ethically proper practices can be developed. After all, most students in the United States before the age of consent are in school by order of the civil law and in this sense great numbers of students are captives. Institutional captivity, I have argued, need not preclude a moral concern with students' freedom and liberty.

The issue of activity-based captivity on the part of experiential educators has an aspect of it that is unique and deserves a bit deeper treatment here. Many situations arise in adventure-based experiential education at the activity level where students are physically held captive, as Ernie was, by ropes and the uniqueness of the situations in which they find themselves. For example, I recently had a group of young people on the Mankato State University High Ropes Course. One young man became quite frightened upon reaching the balance beam 35 feet off the ground. He demanded to be lowered to the ground by the belay rope. His teacher was standing there and told me to hold him up high and not allow him to be lowered. This presented a dilemma. Do I respect the student's wishes, acknowledge his autonomy, and lower him or do I respect the teacher's wishes, deny the student's autonomy, and keep him high on the balance beam? The teacher's motives were benevolent. He wanted the young man to conquer his fears and gain a valuable lesson. This was a classic case of the point at hand. I was in a unique position to keep that young man captive against his wishes so that he might learn a valuable lesson.

One way to address the morality of this sort of activity-based captivity is in terms of the nature of the student-teacher relationship. The relationship of teacher to student is, hopefully, fundamentally different from the relationship of a prison guard to a prisoner. If it is different, how is it different? I suspect that a possible answer to the morality of activity-based captivity of students lies in the uniqueness of the student-teacher relationship as such. The Jewish theologian, Martin Buber, has some words about education that are useful in this context:

Yet the Master remains the model for the teacher. For if the educator of our day has to act consciously he must nevertheless do it "as though he did not." That raising of the finger, that questioning glance, are his genuine doing. Through him the selection of the effective world reaches the pupil. He fails the recipient when he presents this selection to him with a gesture of interference. It must be concentrated in him; and doing out of concentration has the appearance of rest. Interference divides the soul in his care into an obedient part and a rebellious part. But a hidden influence proceeding from his integrity has an integrating force.[1]

The point of this passage is that fundamentally it is the student who is doing the learning. The teacher, as Master, is there to teach "as though he did not." Buber presents an image of the teacher-student relationship as similar to mountain guide and client. The guide shows the way but the client climbs the mountain. The teacher's role is to impel the student into an opportunity for learning. I made the distinction earlier in this chapter between an order and an opportunity. In a sense, when a teacher gives an order to a student, he is doing something fundamentally different than providing an opportunity for the student. Providing an opportunity keeps the student in ultimate control and giving an order places the final control in the hands of the teacher. According to Buber, the teacher should "influence" the student and not be an "interference" to the student. To interfere with a student means to produce a conflict within the student between obedience and rebellion. To influence a student means to aid that student in her search for integration.

For a teacher to suddenly hold a student captive and order her to accomplish a given task is to take the learning away from the student and place it in the hands of the teacher. As John Dewey has written;

The teacher's place and work in the school is to be interpreted from the same basis. **The teacher is not in the school to impose certain ideas or to form certain habits in the child**, *but is there as a member of the community to select influences which will affect the child and to assist him in properly responding to these influences.* [2]

It is arguable that the moment a teacher takes a willing student and, because of the nature of the educational activity, turns her into a captive, the teacher-student relationship has instantly been transformed into a guard-prisoner relationship. A prisoner has no choice but to obey the command. A student has the freedom to reject the ministrations of the teacher.

It is important to remember here that the quotations from Buber and Dewey use words like "selection of the effective world" (Buber), "hidden influence" (Buber), "select influences" (Dewey), "assist him" (Dewey). I am not arguing that teachers in experiential education programs ought not do everything in their educational power to encourage students like Ernie to accomplish more than they think they can accomplish. One of the signs of a skillful teacher is the ability to bring out talents and abilities in students that the students did not know they had. Whenever we, as teachers, "select influences" (Dewey) for our students, we are doing what is expected of us as professionals. The influence that we select may well be a ropes course or a rock climb. However, impelling a willing student into an educationally sound activity is a very different thing from coercively ordering a captive to perform some action against her will.

In the Secrecy chapter, I used Socrates' analogy that the teacher-student relationship is similar to the midwife-patient relationship. That analogy fits nicely in the discussion of captive populations. As recently as 15 years ago in this country, women in childbirth were the passive, docile partners in relationship with an obstetrician. The obstetrician was in charge of childbirth not the woman. Usually, she was drugged, strapped down, and allowed no role in childbirth except as a birthing machine who paid the bill at the end. The woman's partner or husband was banished from the delivery room. In short, the woman was temporarily the captive of the obstetrical profession. Women rebelled against this sort of dependent relationship and demanded that they be willing partners in childbirth with their health-care professionals. Radical changes in the obstetrical practices of this country have been brought about. The woman is in charge, not the midwife or obstetrician. The health professional is there to aid and assist, not coerce and command. If Socrates' analogy is a sound one, then educators might learn some lessons from the changes brought about recently in the child birthing relationships.

It is in this sense that we violate the very foundations of the teacher-student relationship whenever we take a student and turn that student into our captive in order that she attain desired goals. If turning students into captives violates the very foundations of the teacher-student relationship, then it is at least possible that using experiential activities to turn students into captives is unethical in the extreme.

Finally, it is important to note that the examples of captive students, both institutional and activity-based, used in this chapter so far have been fairly obvious examples. The student on a course by court order is an obvious captive. So is the student who becomes a captive during a specific activity. However, many captive-type situations may be present that are far more subtle than the examples used so far. For instance, a young man may be on an experiential education course or program in order to please an overbearing and insecure parent. This young person may desperately need his parent's approval and is willing to submit to almost anything to gain that approval. In a sense, this young man is **dependent** upon his parent's approval and is, therefore, a **captive** to that approval. He may not be acting freely but is, instead, acting under the compulsion of his dependency needs. It seems clear that the issue of freely giving informed consent would be problematic for this person. Practitioners of experiential education ought to be acutely aware of the various subtle influences operating upon students which may render them less than free in their decisions, and, therefore, captive to something. I may be held captive by the court system and I may be held captive by a need for parental approval. The difference is merely one of explicitness.

This could lead into one of the deepest and most difficult of all philosophical problems - free will versus determinism. It is beyond the scope of this book to get into that issue any further. However, it is enough if practitioners realize that dealing with captive students, in whatever form, presents unique and difficult ethical problems.

Chapter Six / Captive Populations

Endnotes / Chapter 6

1. Martin Buber, "Education", in <u>Education and American Culture</u>, ed. Steiner, Arnove, and McClellen (New York: Macmillan Publishing, 1980), 110.

2. John Dewey "My Pedagogic Creed", in <u>The Philosophy of John Dewey</u>, ed. John J. McDermott (Chicago: The University of Chicago Press, 1981), 447.

Chapter Seven

Sexual Issues

Marie and Phil were 19 year-old students on a month-long cultural journalism, experiential education program. They were in a group of young adult students who would be together for the duration of the course. Two instructors were assigned to the group. About day 14 of the course, it became apparent to both Marie and Phil that they were romantically attracted to each other. This attraction manifested itself by sexual behaviors such as hand holding and walking arm-in-arm upon occasion. Marie and Phil began to sleep together. Both students were outstanding participants in the program and both had contributed a great deal to the group. Their outstanding performances both as students and as group members continued after the romantic liaison began. The two instructors met one evening and discussed the situation and wondered together about what, if anything, should be done about Marie and Phil's relationship.

Sue was an experienced and capable wilderness-based experiential educator. She was 28 years old and unmarried. During one of her courses, she had a student named Al who was 30 years old, single, and interested in the possibility of pursuing an outdoor career. As the course went on, Sue and Al began to have long talks together when time permitted. The course was going exceptionally well and Sue and Al began to anticipate their time together alone. It became clear to both of them that there was a romantic attraction. Being mature adults, Sue and Al sat down one evening and discussed their emerging feelings for each other. They decided that they had better be very careful about the emerging romance but they also felt that they could handle sexual expressions of their feelings during those rare moments when they were alone.

Will and Angie were two instructors assigned to instruct an adaptive wilderness program for juvenile delinquents. It was a 42-day-long course. The two of them made a powerful and effective instructional team. The course was going well and they were making significant progress with their students. As they worked together they began to realize that their working relationship was turning into a romantic relationship. As the course went on they began a sexual relationship which seemed to add to their overall appreciation for and interest in the course in general.

These three scenarios just outlined illustrate three aspects of sexuality that are common in many situations of experiential education. The three aspects addressed in this chapter are: Student-student sex; student-teacher sex; and teacher-teacher sex. It seems clear that sexuality manifests itself pervasively in our culture and, therefore, it seems reasonable to assume that it will manifest itself during the professional lives of practitioners. It should be pointed out that there is a peculiar aspect of many experiential education programs that adds to the potential for sexual matters becoming an ethical issue. I am referring to the fact that so many experiential education programs involve long periods of time of living together away from the normal strictures and rules of the culture. Therefore, it is appropriate that practitioners think critically about what some of the moral implications are for sex in their professional lives.

Two alternatives present themselves immediately as possible methods for dealing with sexual issues. These are denial and prohibition.

The human inclination for denial of problems has received a great deal of attention by professionals in the human service occupations. It is a well known adage of chemical dependency treatment, for instance, that denial is the chief obstacle to confronting chemical abuse problems. I argued in the Risk-Benefit chapter of this book that the attempt to run a risk-free wilderness program is a form of psychological denial. My experience with discussing sexual issues has been that oftentimes a type of psychological denial takes place. Practitioners sometimes retort that their students are too interested in learning to have time for sex. Or they say that they have never had to deal with sexual matters and, therefore, such matters are really fictitious. Sometimes denial takes the form of saying that what appears to be sexual behavior is really just "kidding around" or friendly "hugs" that have nothing to do with sex. My contention is that sexual matters are usually present wherever human beings are together. To deny the presence of sexual issues is to deny the intricacies of human nature. As an ethical issue, denial is especially pernicious because it makes it impossible to deal rationally with something that cannot be admitted as real. My contention throughout this book has been that ethical matters must be dealt with rationally. To deny reality is a form of irrationality. Therefore, the denial of the reality of sexual matters in experiential education is a form of irrationality that is antithetical to a rational discussion of sexual ethics.

The second common response to raising sexual issues is the simple prohibition of sex. In the past two years, I have had conversations with several practitioners from different parts of the country, in entirely different types of experiential education programs, who said that their programs deal with sex by prohibiting it completely. This move acknowledges the reality of sex but its response of prohibition simply evades any discussion of the ethics of sexual behavior. To cut off discussing serious ethical matters, while convenient, nevertheless leaves the matter unresolved. Prohibition of sexuality is like a "Now you see it, now you don't" magic trick. More specifically, it is my view that simple prohibition of sexuality is really a subtle form of denial. To prohibit that which is real is like shaking one's fist at a bothersome mosquito. I may feel better after shaking my fist at the mosquito, but unless I confront it directly, it is still buzzing around, waiting to bother me.

The opening example of Marie and Phil presents the issue of students becoming sexually involved with each other. I purposely presented that case because it involves two people over the legal age of consent and it involves a group situation. Cases that involve students who are younger than the age of consent (which varies from state to state in the United States), and which do not involve a larger group of students, require a different ethical analysis than the case of Marie and Phil. What follows immediately below assumes: 1) the students are adults, and 2) they are involved with a larger group. The case of younger students and no group impact is examined after the first case.

At first glance it can be argued that sexual relations between consenting adults are, simply, none of an experiential education practitioner's business at all. One could say that the teacher's job is to teach and since expressions of student sexuality do not involve the teaching function, it is, therefore, beyond the instructor's professional concern. While this appears to be a reasonable premise, it may be false. Many experiential education programs have as a vital aspect of their methodology, the impact of small group living. I recall a newspaper article recently where a group of college students in Minnesota participated in a history class which included living in a pioneer era cabin during two months of the Minnesota winter. They lived exactly as the Swedish settlers did in the 19th century. The article pointed out that the most demanding aspect of the whole course was dealing with the other students and the intense interpersonal relationships that had to be worked out.

To argue that the sole function of that history professor was to teach history using an experiential methodology is false. The students reported that they learned much more than just history. Granted they learned a great deal of history, but they also learned a lot about themselves.

My wife worked as an elementary teacher in the Alabama public schools for seven years. One day one of her most able and cooperative students began to exhibit disruptive behavior. He became totally obnoxious and was affecting the entire classroom. Finally, she pulled the student aside and asked him what was going on. He denied any particular problem. Finally, the day passed and as the other children left the room this little boy stopped by my wife's desk. She asked him, once more, what was happening. His lower lip began to quiver and he sobbed, "My hamster died this morning!"

The illustrations of the history professor and the elementary teacher point out the fact that the teacher's role is not simply to input information. Especially with group situations common to so many experiential education programs, the instructor's educational role is intimately connected with the functioning of the group. It is in this sense that an instructor may have a legitimate concern with student sexuality, even if it involves consenting adults. The concern might not be with sexuality per se. Rather, sexuality is placed in the broader context of the functioning of the group in general. The reasoning is that since the instructor's role is to impel students to learn and since the functioning of the group affects student learning, therefore, the instructor is legitimately concerned with group functioning. Again, it is vital to focus in on the educational significance of the group and not just on sexuality in isolation. Sexuality becomes of concern to instructors when it has an impact of educational significance.

Sexual activity among consenting adult students can have three possible influences on the rest of the group: negative, positive, or neutral. It is easy to imagine possible negative influences of expressions of sexuality on a group's functioning. One negative result that is possible is the problem of student jealousy. Person A is attracted to person B and person C is also attracted to B. B welcomes the affection of person A but spurns person C. C then becomes jealous of A and problems result. The instructor is forced to deal with a dysfunctional group. Another negative consequence can be that the two people involved begin to isolate themselves from participation in the overall educational goals which brought the group together in the first place. Educational goals then become secondary to the goal of pursuit of the sexual relationship.

In the discussion of possible negative consequences of sexuality within a broader group, it is tempting to begin talking about group process and group psychotherapeutic techniques. It is beyond the scope of this book to get into these issues. The concern is with the morality of these issues, not with ameliorative techniques. Morally, it seems to be the case that when sexual expressions begin to interfere with the overall educational goals of the program, with a resulting negative consequence to other students, then the teacher is morally obligated to deal with the issue and prevent further harm.

It is also very possible that a romantic liaison between two students may have a positive influence on the group. The example of Marie and Phil was presented in such a way that their relationship strengthened the two students and their participation in the educational goals of the rest of the group. If this was the case, then an instructor who wanted to intervene in or stop that relationship might have a difficult time ethically justifying the intervention. However, it seems clear that there would be no way for the instructor to know about negative or positive consequences of sexuality unless that instructor was acutely aware of the group's functioning in general. Thus, the demand is placed upon the instructor, as a minimum condition, that he at least be aware of the negative or positive impact.

I raised the possibility of neutral consequences on the educational functioning of the group. My own experience has been that it is a very rare phenomenon where student sexuality is a merely neutral group influence. As a practical matter, it may be that neutral group impact is improbable. Usually any change in the complex web of student relationships will affect the group either negatively or positively. Philosophically, though, neutral impacts are possible. As an ethical matter, it would be the case that a truly neutral impact on the educational goals of the participants would render the sexual relationship irrelevant.

The ethics of student-to-student sex that involves students younger than the age of consent presents special problems and demands a different analysis. Marie and Phil were both 19 years old. How about students who are, say, 15 years old?

The key ethical problem of adolescent sexuality revolves around the notions of consent, personal autonomy, and in loco parentis. The reason that adult students who become sexually involved with each other presents a far different issue than adolescent students is because it is assumed that adults can give autonomous consent. Whether or not younger students can give consent is a root problem behind hesitations of allowing adolescent sexual relations while on experiential education programs. Another source of the ethically problematic nature of adolescent sexuality is the issue of the adolescent's teacher serving the role of a parent while a student is under the teacher's care. The term used to signify the surrogate parenting role of an instructor is "in loco parentis," which means "in the position or place of a parent." It is useful to separate the two notions of autonomous consent and in loco parentis.

The reason rape is morally repugnant is because it involves a violation of the free will and autonomy of the person being raped. No consent is given in a rape. Therefore, rape is unethical. Many people opposed to adolescent expressions of sexuality apply a similar reasoning process. This application argues that non-consensual sex is unethical. In order to give consent one must be autonomous. Adolescents may think they are autonomous, the reasoning goes, but they are mistaken and the program must protect them from their faulty thinking. This is a highly controversial aspect of ethical theory and of the law. It is controversial because the premise of the argument (that adolescents are not autonomous) may not be true. The United States Supreme Court and legal scholars are in violent disagreement over the issue of adolescent autonomy, as evidenced by recent litigation involving adolescent access to contraceptives and abortion without parental approval.

As thus far presented, the issue has been cast in either-or terms which allow for no variability among individuals. It may well be the case that some adolescents are capable of autonomous consent. If it is the case that some adolescents are capable of autonomous consent, then it is at least possible that some adolescents on experiential education programs are capable of ethically acceptable sexual expressions. The problem, then, for instructors is discerning and judging which individuals are capable of autonomous decision making and which are not. I suspect that the reason so many programs outright prohibit adolescent expressions of sexuality is because of the difficulty of making the judgments of who is autonomous and who is not. Instructors are, therefore, put in an ethical dilemma. If they prohibit adolescent sexual expressions completely, they may well be casting a too broad categorical net that does ethical violence to those who are capable of autonomous decision making. On the other hand, if they permit responsible sexual expressions, they have the burden of determining who is responsible and who is not.

The issue of the in loco-parentis-role of teachers is another way of approaching the adolescent sexuality issue. I recently spoke with a young mother about this issue. She told me that if she had a son or daughter on an experiential education program, she would be outraged if she were to discover that her child was sexually involved with another student with the instructor's knowledge and permission. In other words, she felt that the program had a moral obligation to serve a surrogate parent role and enforce certain moral standards that the parents held. This is a compelling argument but it has problems. What comes to mind immediately is the case of an instructor having ten different students under his care and at the same time trying to maintain ten different sets of moral standards of ten different sets of parents!! The spectacle that could result from this seems fairly obvious.

One way out of this would be to maintain the in loco-parentis stance and base it, not on the specific parents involved but, instead, on a broader "community standard" approach. This would be quite utilitarian in nature in that it would ask what most parents would want for their adolescent sons and daughters. The program and instructors could proceed with their policies based upon this standard. As with most utilitarian arguments, the problem then arises about those parents whose standards do not necessarily fit the "community standard." What about their in loco parentis interests? Should their interests be violated just because of a "community standard" adopted by a particular instructor or program? Clearly, the "community standard" approach, while possibly better than the separate standards of every parent involved, itself presents problems.

The second case illustrated in the opening of this chapter raised the issue of sexual relations between instructors and their students. Both were over the age of consent, and both were, therefore, autonomous, consenting adults. Was this sexual relationship a moral one?

As has happened so often in this book, my approach to the issue of instructor-student sexual relations is rooted in the context of the very nature of the student-teacher relationship as such. What is it that makes a student-teacher relationship different from other human relationships? A patient enters into a relationship with the physician in order that the patient be healed. The penitent goes to the priest in order to be forgiven for his sins. It is my contention that a student enters into a relationship with a teacher in order to move from ignorance to knowledge. The fundamental aspect of the student-teacher relationship is that it is entered into in the quest for knowledge. The student-teacher relationship is not simply an I-Thou relationship. There is a third element always present in every teacher-student relationship and that element is a subject matter of some sort. Educational philosopher David Hawkins has written that the thing which sets the student-teacher relationship apart is the presence of a subject matter - an It - which transcends the I-Thou relationship. According to Hawkins, merely having an I-Thou relationship is not sufficient for an educational relationship. The subject matter completes the tripartite relationship. Hawkins writes:

So the first act in teaching, it seems to me, the first goal, necessary to all others, is to encourage this kind of engrossment. Then the child comes alive for the teacher as well as the teacher for the child. They have a common theme for discussion, they are involved together in the world.[1]

Notice that the "engrossment" is not with each other, as in an I-Thou relationship. The teacher and student are engrossed with the world about them - the It - and not exclusively with each other.

Martin Buber has written that since the teacher is not ignorant and since the student is ignorant, their relationship can never be one of complete mutual inclusion. They have a difference of perspective on the subject matter at hand and on each other. As Buber says:

But however intense the mutuality of giving and taking with which he is *bound to his pupil, inclusion cannot be mutual in this case. He experiences the pupil's being educated, but the pupil cannot experience the educating of the educator. The educator stands at both ends of the common situation, the pupil only at one end. In the moment when the pupil is able to throw himself across and experience from over there, **the educative relation would be burst asunder**, or change to friendship.* [2]

Since the relationship is one that is not between equals, it is arguable that there exists a difference in power between student and teacher. The teacher is not ignorant and the student is ignorant. That is why they came together. Once the concern with the move from ignorance to knowledge has been replaced by other concerns, the student-teacher relationship has been violated and radically altered. Buber draws from the doctor-patient relationship to illustrate this point:

*Consider, for example, the relation of doctor and patient. It is essential that this should be a real human relation experienced with the spirit by the one who is addressed; but as soon as the helper is touched by the desire - in however subtle form - to dominate or to enjoy his patient, or to treat the latter's wish to be dominated or enjoyed by him other than as a wrong condition needing to be cured, **the danger of a falsification arises,** beside which all quackery appears peripheral.* [3]

The key words in this quote are "the danger of a falsification arises." For anything which interferes with the move from ignorance to knowledge on the part of the student renders that relationship no longer a student-teacher relationship.

The morality of student-teacher sexual relationships must be examined in terms of the core purpose of that relationship. My own position is that anything that interferes with the I-Thou-It relationship does violence to that relationship. Fundamental to sexual relationships is the supreme importance of the I-Thou relationship. In the case of student and teacher the I-Thou-It has been replaced by I and Thou. Therefore, it seems antithetical to the teacher-student relationship that there be a sexual aspect to that relationship. It is in this sense that student-teacher sexual relationships may be considered unethical in the extreme.

One objection to my argument might be that a couple like Sue and Al could separate those times when they are involved with an I-Thou relationship and when they are in an I-Thou-It relationship. It might well be the case that Sue is not always teaching Al and that when she is done teaching him for the day, they could shift gears, so to speak. Theoretically at least, this seems like a possibility. As a psychological matter, it seems like a gargantuan task to ask people to make the radical shift between their relationship as lovers and their relationship as student and teacher. This difficulty would be especially acute if the shift continually went back and forth on a long-term program. The human propensity for self-deception should be kept in mind in this matter.

The final issue concerns sexual relationships between instructors while working with students. The third example of Will and Angie in the beginning of this chapter illustrated the issue. These instructors were consenting adults and they were not in a student-teacher relationship. Therefore, it could be an easy move to dismiss that relationship as ethically irrelevant. My point of departure, as an ethical matter, is to ask what the primary purpose was which brought Will and Angie together in the first place. They were there to teach. In the analysis of Marie and Phil (both consenting adult students), I suggested that the morality of the relationship had to be examined in light of its impact on the educational goals of the program and on its impact on the rest of the students. A similar reasoning process can be applied to sexual relations between staff members. If Will and Angie are there to teach, then it is reasonable to ask what impact their relationship had on their professional obligations to function as teachers. It is arguable that anything which interferes with a teacher's obligation to function professionally with his students, can be condemned as immoral. Therefore, if the sexual relationship interferes with the instructor's concentration on the student's learning, then it may be wrong.

Logically speaking, there is no reason to draw a direct inference from sexual expressions between teachers to neglect of one's teaching duties. To argue that Will and Angie are sexually involved, therefore they are neglecting their students seems false. However, their relationship may be detracting from their absorption with their students. If it is detracting, then it should be viewed as ethically suspect. As with the issue of teacher-student sexuality, the human tendency to self-deception must be plugged into the ethical analysis. This is where ethics can benefit from psychology. The staff members involved with each other may really believe that they are primarily concerned with their students and not with their own romance. They could be deceiving themselves, however, and this possibility should always be kept in mind.

I am aware of a few situations where the issue of staff members and their romantic liaisons with each other has become the subject of administrative practices which border on absurdity. In the quest to root out instructor engrossment with each other rather than their students, arbitrary cutoff points have been established. For instance, if a couple has been together for X amount of time, then that is long enough to permit them to work together with students. However, if they have been together X-1, then they cannot work together. This sort of micro-managing and judging of staff members' sexual relationships is ethically troubling because it may well constitute unethical intrusions on instructors' personal liberty and autonomy with no clear reason for doing so. It may well be the case that the burden of proof should rest on administrators to prove that a problem exsists with the staff members' relationships, rather than putting this burden on the staff members to prove that there is no problem. Concern with student welfare need not result in unethical intrusions on staff autonomy and liberty.

Finally, I need to say a word about the key role of informed consent on the ethics of sexuality issue. An assumption I have had throughout this chapter is that nothing particular has been said about sexuality prior to beginning the educational endeavor. I think the whole analysis shifts dramatically if everyone involved in the program (adults, adolescents, teachers, students) has agreed beforehand to certain sexual rules. I can imagine a fundamentalist Christian program, for instance, that forbids any and all expressions of sexuality outside of marriage. It could be the case that everyone knew beforehand what these rules were and that sexuality is subsumed under the guidance of agreed-to rules. Therefore, the whole issue of sexual ethics becomes an issue of sexual rules. If this is the case, then the concern is with giving informed consent to abide by the rules.

The same could be said about the issue of staff members. Programs may want to decide that as a condition of employment no sexual expressions between staff members are permissible. Were this to be the case, then this policy would need to be made clear to staff members prior to being hired, if informed consent were to be taken seriously.

Endnotes / Chapter 7

1. David Hawkins "I, Thou, and It" in The Informed Vision, by David Hawkins (New York: Agathon Press, 1974), 57.

2. Martin Buber, "Education," in Education and American Culture, ed. Steiner, Arnove and McClellan (New York: MacMillan, 1980), 118.

3. Buber, "Education," 114

Environmental Concerns

Sammy was a 21-year old man on an extended biology field trip sponsored by his college. He was disabled, having become paraplegic due to an automobile accident. The biology trip was into a wilderness area that had rigid rules governing minimum environmental impact. One afternoon Sammy lost bladder and bowel control, thereby severely soiling himself. He was horrified and begged the biology instructor to place him beside a stream so that he could clean himself off in privacy and retain whatever dignity he had left. He wanted some water bottles and he wanted the rest of the group and the instructor to leave immediately. Realizing that complying with Sammy's wishes would possibly, even probably, result in some human waste entering the stream, the biologist was faced with an ethical dilemma. Should she respect Sammy's wishes or should she follow the rules of minimum impact and deny Sammy's request?

A group of recovering alcoholics were on a 15-day wilderness course designed to aid them in their recovery process. It was winter and severely cold. The group had encountered several days of a blizzard, were wet, discouraged, and ready to quit the course. In keeping with the goal of minimum environmental impact, the group had used no fires on the course, choosing instead to use gasoline stoves for cooking. The instructor was approached by several group members, who requested that they be allowed to build a large fire so that they could have some external heat and dry out their belongings. The instructor knew that the fire would help restore their sagging spirits but she also knew that a fire scar would result if the fire were built. She hesitated in her reply to the group, wondering what was the right thing to do.

Before proceeding further with the discussion of the ethics of environmental concerns, it is useful to bracket out some conceptual parameters. The subject of environmental ethics is so broad and complex as to defy a thorough

Chapter Eight / Environmental Concerns

treatment in one chapter of this book. Therefore, some selections must be made in terms of priorities. **My concern is with the issue of when an environmental value conflicts with a human value.** So often the topic of environmental ethics leads directly into discussions of minimum impact camping techniques, theories of ecology, and the politics of environmental protection. Those issues are not my concern in this chapter.

I take it as an assumption that attempts to preserve the environment are useful and good. I also assume that readers of this book are aware of the various techniques of leading groups of students through environmentally sensitive areas, with minimum impact on those environments. The target audience is not people who need convincing that environmental concerns are valid and worthy of attention. The audience I have in mind are those who are already convinced about the worth of environmentally sound practices but who are nevertheless confronted with **conflicts of values** between human concerns and environmental concerns. The assumption is that practitioners of experiential education who use the natural world as a teaching medium will inevitably encounter conflicts similar to the two examples at the opening of this chapter. Therefore, the goal of this chapter is to sort out what these conflicts of value involve in terms of the moral worth of decisions that might be made.

A useful move is to ask what the reasons might be that would guide an instructor's decision in a case like Sammy. Suppose the instructor were to say **yes** to Sammy. What ethical justifications could be made in defense of that decision?

Fundamental to acquiescing to Sammy's request might be a concern with preserving his dignity and personal autonomy. It could be argued that Sammy's request to bathe by the stream is one that is in his own best interest as defined by himself. Furthermore, Sammy is not deluded about his own best interests, is rational, and is not confusing interests, needs, and wants. What Sammy wants (to bathe himself in privacy) is congruent with his needs (to be cleaned of his own waste) and his interest (to retain his dignity). Therefore, Sammy places a high value on retaining his dignity and personal autonomy. Given Sammy's high value placed on retaining his ability to bathe himself, it could be argued that it would be highly unethical for his instructor not to agree to Sammy's request. The moral judgment might be that, all things being equal, it is better not to compromise the purity of a stream. In this case, however, all things are not equal. Sammy's need for autonomy possibly outweighs the stream's need not to be polluted.

This raises a key distinction that should be kept clear in the type of environmental ethics conflict at hand. In what sense can a non-human stream possibly "**need** not to be polluted?" Can a stream have a need, even though it is not a conscious being? The distinction has already been made in this book in the Deception chapter between the notions of interest, need, and want. These notions were used to describe Sammy's needs, wants, and interests immediately above. These same distinctions are helpful in gaining more clarity in the problem of the stream needing not to be polluted by Sammy's washing.

The notions of want and interest are applicable only to conscious beings. What I want and what I have an interest in may not be good for me, but I consciously want or have an interest. Recall my example in the Deception chapter about the drunkard who has an interest in and wants to drive an automobile at high speeds while he is drunk. I argued there that what he really needed was contrary to what he consciously had an interest in and wanted. In other words, his real needs were not dependent upon his conscious wants and interests. This same line of reasoning can be applied to a stream. It seems silly to say that a stream wants or has an interest in staying clean. However, one could argue that the stream needs to stay clean whether or not it is conscious of this need. For example, my automobile needs oil in the crankcase in order not to burn up. Again, however, it would be silly to suggest that my car is conscious of its need in the form of expressed interests or wants or in any other form. Still, it really does need oil.

This leads directly into a moral argument that could be mustered to **deny** Sammy's request that he be allowed to pollute the stream. The instructor could readily acknowledge Sammy's wants, needs, and interests but could reply that Sammy's need, while real, does not necessarily outweigh the streams' needs. This is the core issue in this formulation of the conflict of value between Sammy and the stream. The instructor must evaluate the conflicting values presented by Sammy and the stream.

If a being or a thing or an ecosystem for that matter, has a genuine need, then it seems reasonable to argue that to deprive that being, thing, or ecosystem of what it needs is to **injure** it. Denial of a need is to injure. However, does it make sense to speak of injuring something that is not capable of conscious experience? Environmental ethicist Scott Lehmann has written about this matter:

The principle is roughly that only what matters or could matter to a thing can injure or benefit it, and the only things to which anything can matter are subjects of experience. If something has no capacity for suffering or enjoyment, no possibility of happiness or misery, no desires to be thwarted or satisfied, no ideals to be respected or dishonored, then it is very hard to see how anything can be accounted injury to it. But all of these features presuppose consciousness.[1]

Lehmann's point is that only a being which is capable of conscious experience can truly be said to suffer an injury. If this line of reasoning is true, then Sammy, being a conscious entity, would have a valid claim to being injured by the denial of his need; while the stream, not being conscious, would have no claim to being injured. Therefore, the stream would have no claim which would override Sammy.

To give the moral nod to Sammy, based on the argument of the priority of conscious beings over nonconscious beings in terms of injury, could collapse the argument if it could be shown that the stream is conscious and can, therefore, suffer real injury. John Muir, one of the fountainheads of modern environmental ethics, suggests that even inanimate objects may possess consciousness:

Now it never seems to occur to these far-seeing teachers that Natures object in making animals and plants might possibly be first of all **the happiness of each one of them**, *not the creation of all for the happiness of one.*

-and later-

Plants are credited with but dim and uncertain sensation, and minerals with positively none at all. But why may not even a mineral arrangement of matter be endowed with sensation of a kind that we in our blind exclusive perfection can have no manner of communication with? [2]

It is a short move to go from ascribing "happiness" and "sensation" to plants and minerals to, therefore, claiming that plants and minerals have consciousness. If a plant or a mineral can be happy, then why not the stream that has a valuational conflict with Sammy? Following this line of reasoning one could conclude that allowing Sammy to clean himself off by the stream could cause the stream injury.

My own view is that it is preposterous to argue that rocks and streams have consciousness in the same way that Sammy has consciousness. It seems that the burden of proof would lie with those who would ascribe consciousness to inanimate objects. Therefore, those who would argue that a stream's interests override those interests of Sammy are faced with a difficult task at best.

There is another line of reasoning that could be used to deny Sammy's request that would not require that one believe in the consciousness of inanimate objects. The instructor could reason that Sammy's interests in preserving his dignity and autonomy must be weighed against the claims of the interests of other people that the stream not be polluted. **The conflict of value would be between Sammy and the interests of other people, not between Sammy and the stream itself.** The shift from discussion of the interests of the stream to the interests of other people in the stream's purity is illustrated from a legal example. Environmental ethicist Jay Kantor gives the example of law suits involving pollution:

*Suits involving **natural objects** - such things as trees, streams, forests, and lakes, or ecological systems which involve a balance of conditions among, for* *example, a lake, a stream that feeds the lake, plants and animals within the stream and lake, and plants and animals in the area surrounding the stream and lake - have traditionally focused on the effects of "tampering" with these natural objects upon human interests. Thus, a company dumping pollutants into a stream may be sued by a farmer downstream for damage he or his property suffers as a result of the pollution. The stream itself has no legal standing, no rights in the matter.* ³

It is the farmer whose interests were violated in the above quote, not the stream.

The move to root the stream's value in the interests of other people rather than in its own interests presents one of the most difficult and still unresolved issues in environmental ethics. Is it possible that nature has **inherent value**, apart from any use, appreciation, or worth to human beings? It is not very controversial to argue that Sammy has inherent value due to his status as a person. It is quite controversial to argue that streams have inherent value in and of themselves. Environmental ethicist Tom Regan goes so far as to say that the issue of inherent value in nature is the pivotal issue for even the possibility of an environmental ethic:

But more fundamentally, there is the earlier question about the very possibility of an environmental ethic. If I am right, the development of what can properly be called an environmental ethic requires that we postulate inherent value in nature. ⁴

The jury is still out on whether or not it makes sense to talk of nature having inherent value. While it is tempting to go into more detail about this theoretical issue, it would be beyond the scope of this book to get any further into that issue. For suppose nature does have inherent value. That would not necessarily resolve the issue of Sammy. **Inherent value** does not necessarily entail a commitment to **equal value**. The conflict would remain between Sammy's value and the stream's value even if they both have inherent value.

This leads directly back to the argument that the stream has value to other people and that the other people's interests should be part of the instructor's decision. One way to go would be to examine one of the assumptions of the argument thus far presented. I have assumed that the stream is either 1) polluted or 2) not polluted by Sammy. No room has been made for a middle ground between the either-or formulation. It is possible that the interest of other people not to have a polluted stream can be protected and that Sammy can maintain his dignity without polluting the stream very much. It is at least possible that the environmental impact of Sammy's washing himself will be so transitory and minimal that the interests of others in a pure stream will not be compromised enough to raise a strong objection.

Chapter Eight / Environmental Concerns

This is where consequential and nonconsequential ethical positions become very helpful. An ethical nonconsequentialist might well find the calculation of the degree of pollution irrelevant to the discussion. I can imagine the instructor of the group declaring that it is **never acceptable** to pollute a stream even a little bit, even if it results in good consequences for Sammy. Good consequences to Sammy and minor negative consequences to the purity of the stream would not be enough to sway this instructor's decision. She would have to deny Sammy's request if she were a true ethical nonconsequentialist.

An ethical consequentialist might well take the opposite view and reason that given the good consequences for Sammy and the minor negative consequences to the stream's purity, that the right thing to do would be to grant Sammy's request. An alternative consequentialist move would be to try to determine the degree of potential harm and benefit to both Sammy and other people and then act accordingly. Sammy's interests might well lose out to the interests of other people in this scenario.

Something that ethically concerned experiential education practitioners might do to deal with cases like Sammy's would be to decide beforehand how they stand on environmental issues and the conflict of values these issues present. Once these decisions were reached, potential participants could be informed beforehand what the environmental stakes are. For instance, a paraplegic like Sammy who might lose bowel and bladder control could be forewarned that his need for dignity either would or would not take precedence over environmental concerns. The issue would then convert to an informed consent issue.

This is especially important with programs which deal with student populations with disabilities or sensitivities that would frequently raise environmental conflicts of value. The case of a group of physically disabled students is relevant. A hard-core environmentalist (nonconsequentialist) might be nervous about taking these people into environmentally sensitive areas. One could go two ways here. One could be to simply inform group members **before the fact** that their disabilities (bladder, bowel control primarily) are not justification enough ever to compromise minimum impact values. Another move would be to tell them that everything possible will be done to protect their dignity even if it involves some compromise with minimum impact values.

The second example in the beginning of the chapter about the recovering alcoholics presents conflicts of value involving environmental issues that are a bit different from the case of Sammy. In the alcoholic's case, the instructor was considering building a fire in order to increase the students' general well being and not primarily because of an issue of dignity and autonomy, as in Sammy's case. In addition, there was more than one person involved. The issue can be focused into the question of whether improving the general welfare of a group of students justifies compromises of environmental values.

One argument that can be made in response to this problem is to say that **any** intrusion by human beings into a protected wilderness area is going to have an impact on that area, however minimal it may be. For the strict preservationist who demands zero impact and not just minimal impact, it would be reasonable to conclude that no human use should be permitted. It is arguable that zero impact is an impossibility. Simply by walking on the ground, the turf is compacted and foot marks are left. Breathing the air alters the atmosphere ever so slightly. Splashing through a stream alters that stream's flow even for a few seconds. The point is that if zero impact on wilderness is the goal, then it seems reasonable that the only way to attain that is to simply keep people out completely. There are environmentalists who argue exactly this way. If this position were taken, then the problem of the alcoholics and their fire would evaporate, since they would not be there in the first place.

The other argument would be to eschew the goal of zero impact and, instead, have a goal of minimum impact. This is an ethical move of major importance because it lets human interests become the determining factor in whether to alter the environment. The position is that since great gains will be attained by people encountering wilderness, that human impact is ethically justified. Granted, the proviso is added that impact by people will be kept to a minimum. Then the question becomes one of the degrees of environmental impact and the degrees of human gain.

Once a proportion is established between the level of human benefit and the level of environmental impact, then a possible solution to cases like the alcoholics might emerge. In the Risk/Benefit chapter I presented the possibility of ethically justifying risky educational activities by the amount of benefit to be gained. More benefit might justify more risk. One could substitute the words "environmental impact" for risk and do an identical reasoning process. It is at least possible that greater impact on the environment is justified only when a great deal of human benefit can be shown. It is arguable that the recovering alcoholics stand to gain enormous benefit by entering the wilderness area and that the benefit justifies entering the area in the first place. This reasoning does not resolve the issue of the fire after the blizzard. It could be argued that the benefit to the participants justifies nothing more than entering the wilderness with a pledge to keep impact to a minimum. The building of the fire raises the stakes of the proportion on the side of environmental value. Clearly, the fire will create a greater environmental impact than if no fire had been built. The ethical problem for the instructor on the scene is whether there is a corresponding benefit to be gained which will offset the environmental impact.

As that example was presented, there was an aspect of the example that is very relevant to the ethics of the instructor's decision. It can be argued that a program which sends out a group of recovering alcoholics in the middle of winter in a cold climate without some sort of external heat source is guilty of dereliction of duty. In other words, someone opposed to building the fire on ethical grounds could argue that the group should have had a wall tent with a stone in it, just for situations like blizzards and extreme cold. It is possible that environmental impact issues like the one presented should never have come up in the first place had the instructor prepared her course properly from the beginning. Therefore, the moral onus would rest upon the shoulders of those who improperly planned the course. If the students' need for a fire were denied, it could be defended as not really based upon the competing claim of environmental minimum impact, but upon the poor planning of the program or instructor.

This move of shifting the discussion from ethics to poor planning, while attractive, leaves the fundamental conflict of value unresolved. Suppose the program had provided a wall tent with a stove in it and the tent blew away in the blizzard, thereby rendering the little stove worthless. What then? In other words, it is very easy to imagine scenarios where the planning reflected ethical concern for environmental impact but something intervenes which renders the best intended planning useless. Regardless of the efforts to maintain minimum impact, the instructor is saddled with a group of cold, debilitated students who really do need an external heat source. Should she build the fire?

This leads directly back to the proportion of benefit to impact. I have stressed throughout this book the importance of making value judgments. This case demands that the instructor judge which value will win out in her decision. Her judgment, in order to be rational, must be made with clear understanding of what the levels of benefit and impact probably are. She cannot know for certain before the fact what the benefits to the group will be if the fire is built. But she can, as a rational being, have at least some idea of what the benefits might be. Similarly, she cannot know for sure what negative impact the fire will have on the environment in the long run. But, she can have at least some idea of the possible impacts. Her judgment, in order to be a moral one, must reflect her having weighed the competing values and having considered the possible benefits to the students and potential impact on an environment that other people (not on the scene) value being minimally impacted.

Endnotes / Chapter 8

1. Scott Lehmann, "Do Wildernesses Have Rights?" The Journal of Environmental Ethics 3, no. 2 (Summer 1981), 137.

2. John Muir, The Wilderness World of John Muir ed. Edwin Way Teale (Boston: Houghton Mifflin Co., 1976), 317.

3. Jay E. Kantor, "The 'Interests' of Natural Objects," in The Journal of Environmental Ethics 2, no. 2 (Summer 1980), 164.

4. Tom Regan, "The Nature and Possibility of an Environmental Ethic," in The Journal of Environmental Ethics 3, no. 1 (Spring 1981), 34.

Chapter Nine

Individual Versus Group Benefit

Cindy was a 17-year-old girl on a 23-day wilderness-based experiential education program. She was in a group of nine other students from many different areas of the United States. From the beginning of the program, Cindy had been having problems with the physical aspects of the course due to the fact that she was quite overweight. For instance, during group initiative exercises, she was unable to be of much help to the group and the biggest single problem the group had to solve was how to get Cindy through the problems. She could not hike very far with a backpack without becoming thoroughly exhausted. As the course progressed, the group figured out ways to help Cindy, like distributing her load among the other, stronger group members. When she first came on the course, her attitude had been terrible. She was belligerent and resentful of the abilities of the other students. As time went on, her attitude improved considerably and she began to show signs of dramatic psychological and interpersonal growth. She was becoming an accepted member of the group.

Sandy and Rachel were in the same group with Cindy. Both Sandy and Rachel had been athletes in college and high school and both were physically fit. Throughout their athletic endeavors, neither Sandy nor Rachel had ever dealt with serious fear and neither had pushed their limits to the utmost. The reason they had come on the experiential education program was to push some of the limits that they had never pushed before.

As the course went on, Sandy and Rachel began to resent all of the attention that Cindy had been getting. They confided their concerns to the instructors, who listened supportively and urged them to work with Cindy and make the best of a difficult situation.

On day 15 of the course, the group was scheduled to do a climb of a large, snow-covered mountain. The day before the climb was to begin, the instructors got the group together and explained the details of the forthcoming climb. Part of the climb would involve kicking steps in deep snow on steep slopes. It was going to be a difficult climb but one that many other groups had successfully climbed.

During the discussion several of the group members, following the leadership of Sandy and Rachel, asked Cindy if she would consider staying at the base camp that day, as it seemed clear that Cindy would be unable to complete the climb. Cindy replied that she had as much right to attempt the climb as the other group members and that she wanted to try the climb. The instructor pointed out that, as a safety matter, if one person had to turn back, then the whole group would have to turn back. A long discussion ensued and the group was unable to reach a consensus of what to do. The group was evenly split on whether Cindy should attempt the climb, with Cindy being very clear about her desire to attempt the climb. Therefore, the group asked the instructors to make the decision for them and everyone agreed to abide by the instructors' decision.

The problem of group versus individual benefit is one of the most persistent and vexing ethical issues in education in general and in experiential education in particular. The conflict in value between Cindy, Rachel and Sandy and the rest of the group is typical of the conflict between individual and group benefits that practitioners frequently encounter.

Since the issue of individual versus group benefit always arises within the context of a group setting, it is often tempting to convert the ethical conflict into a group psychological conflict, resolvable by deft and sensitive group process techniques. In the case of Cindy versus the group, the instructor could try and show the group that the real testing of their limits would lie in their ability to adapt to Cindy's limitations. Although Sandy and Rachel **thought** their limits resided in the physical realm, the real testing for them would be in learning to delay or deny their own gratifications and learn the difficult lesson of compassion for Cindy. The instructor's role, therefore, would be to serve as an effective group facilitator. The goal would be to convert the other group members from their previous beliefs of what constituted a benefit for themselves.

The other way for the instructor to turn the ethical conflict into a psychological one would be to try and rechannel Cindy's goals in another direction. Cindy may have thought that she needed to attempt the peak climb but what she really needed to do was to learn the lesson of compassion for her fellows who had already sacrificed so much for her benefit. The instructor's role would be to help Cindy realize that her beliefs about what was in her own best interest were mistaken.

Either of these solutions constitute what I mean by trying to psychologize the ethical issue away. Granted, it could be convenient, even psychologically growthful, if either Cindy or the rest of the group would change their thinking about the issue. Such a change would solve the conflict at hand and would allow the group and Cindy to function well together. My speculation is that many conflicts between group and individual benefit can, indeed, be dealt with by sophisticated psychology on the part of the staff. An instructor who can show an individual or a group that what they had thought was beneficial was not really beneficial and replace the mistaken benefit with a genuine benefit, should be applauded as an expert professional.

There are situations, however, that involve individual versus group benefit that are not solvable by good psychology. Suppose that what the group believes is beneficial, really is in their best interest. Suppose, also, that what Cindy believes is in her best interest really is in her best interest and that **no amount of group process skill on the part of the instructor will resolve these conflicts of value.** This is where the ethical issue presents itself.

In my experience as a practitioner, the most common way of dealing with group versus individual benefit conflicts is through some formulation of the utilitarian calculus. At first glance, it seems reasonable that the only morally right thing to do when such conflicts of value arise is to apply the criterion of maximizing the greatest good for the greatest number. In the case of Cindy versus the group, it is easy to imagine the instructor reasoning that the high benefit to the group attained by requiring that Cindy stay in base camp is enough to justify overriding her wishes.

This same line of reasoning is widely practiced in educational policy decisions involving a much wider scope than just experiential education. For instance, a school district must decide how to spend $50,000.00. The choice is between an accelerated program for the top 10% of the students or a regular program for the middle 30% of the students. Very often such decisions are made with the value that it is better to benefit more students with lower abilities than less students with higher abilities.

Just the opposite reasoning can be applied. One could argue that it is better to take those with the highest abilities and ensure that they go as far as possible in order to achieve the highest benefit for those most able. Furthermore, this line of reasoning can summon a utilitarian argument to support its case. It can be argued that by allowing the most capable, few though they may be, to achieve a high level of benefit, everyone else will benefit by having these high achievers around because of the great contributions they will make to the greater good.

The word **need** can be substituted for the word ability in the ethical analysis. In the case of Cindy, one could argue that her need was so great that her claim to attempt the climb outweighed the lesser needs of Sandy and Rachel. The reverse could be argued: that it is better to supply the lesser needs

Chapter Nine / Individual Versus Group Benefit

of the greater number of students than to focus in too much on the solitary needs of Cindy.

While the utilitarian approach to conflicts between individual versus group benefit is common and sometimes useful, severe problems are inherent in this solution to the problem. Throughout this book, I have pointed out the problem of protecting the interests of those who do not belong to the greatest number in terms of benefit. It is easy to imagine the utilitarian calculus degenerating down a slippery slope of complete disregard for the solitary individual or minority whose interests are at variance with the greatest number.

One way of approaching the issue is to cast it as a question of **fairness**. In terms of Cindy, Sandy and Rachel, the issue could be outlined as a problem of fairness. Given all the sacrifices made by the group to Cindy, is it fair for Cindy to make the claim for attempting the climb, knowing full well that her participation would likely preclude any of the other students from finishing? Similarly, is it fair to deny Cindy her wish just because the others were claiming their due?

One way of dealing with the fairness issue as it relates to individual versus group benefit in experiential education is to tie it in with the goals of the program and students having given informed consent to those goals. When a student has entered a given experiential education program, it seems reasonable that he has agreed to function in accord with the goals of that program once his informed consent has been freely given. It is arguable that certain goals imply certain rules. If my goal in joining a football team is to play football, then I am obligated to follow the rules of football. Suppose I fumble the ball and another player gains possession. I then look at the referee with a plaintive gaze and explain that I really need to recover the ball because my whole self-worth depends on it. If the referee were to grant my wish, then he would be violating the very structure which makes the game of football what it is. The referee could reply that I freely chose to play football and **that I agreed to play by rules that were fair to all players**. Therefore, I would be unreasonable in my desire to have my fumbled ball returned to me.

A similar reasoning process could be applied to the example in the beginning of this chapter. The question should be asked if all of the students had agreed to the goals of the program and thereby agreed to follow certain rules that were fair to all. It might well have been the case that the goal of the program was to allow **all** of the students to test their physical limits. If this had been the case, then it would be unfair to the rest of the group to deny them access to the same challenges enjoyed by Cindy exclusively. On the other hand, the goal of the program might have been to have every activity at least attempted by every member of the group functioning as a group. If this was the case, then there

Chapter Nine / Individual Versus Group Benefit

might have existed a rule requiring that in cases like Cindy's she be permitted to attempt the climb.

One question that arises is the problem of determining whether a given institution or program has fair rules. By what criteria is fairness judged? Philosopher John Rawls has written a great deal about fairness as it relates to individual and group benefit. An institution is a just institution, according to Rawls, when it meets two criteria:

First: each person is to have an equal right to the most extensive basic liberty compatible with a similar liberty for others. Second: social and economic inequalities are to be arranged so that they are both A) reasonably expected to be to everyone's advantage, and B) attached to positions and offices open to all.[1]

The first criterion means that everyone in the group has equal **access** to the goals of the educational program. The second criterion means that if there must exist unequal **attainment** of the educational goals by different students, it is permissible only if the other students benefit by the unequal attainment and that everyone has at least the possibility open to him of attempting his maximum attainment. To have access to something and to actually be successful in attaining something are different notions. The educational program could be called a just program if it meets these two criteria.

Once students are in a just educational program, they are obligated to play fairly by the rules. The next question that must be answered is, what are the criteria of fairness to which the students must adhere? Rawls refers to a possible criterion of fairness that is very useful to the conflict between Cindy and the rest of her group:

*The main idea is that when a number of persons engage in a mutually advantageous cooperative venture according to rules, and thus restrict their liberty in ways necessary to yield advantages for all, those who have submitted to these restrictions have a right to a similar acquiescence on the part of those who have benefited from their submission. **We are not to gain from the cooperative labors of others without doing our fair share.***[2]

Drawing from Rawls, it seems clear that a program which had as part of its rules the notion that only one or else a few students were free to press their limits, would violate the first criterion for a just program. Also, a program that allowed only one or a few students to attain the benefits of having pushed their limits with no corresponding benefit to the others would violate the second criterion of a just program. Furthermore, for a student to ask her fellows to sacrifice their freedom to push their limits and never to return the favor would be to violate the criteria of fairness outlined immediately above. Therefore, the argument could be made that Cindy, in her demand that the other students constantly sacrifice for her, **with no corresponding sacrifice on her part on**

their behalf, was violating the most basic principles of fairness.

As originally formulated, the conflict between Cindy and the group was presented without reference to any previously agreed-to rules which governed fairness in the achievement of the program's educational goals. In a sense, the instructors, Cindy, and her fellow students were operating in a moral vacuum in terms of what constituted fairness. No informed consent had been given about what the rules of the game actually were. Therefore, no one knew anything about what moral principles should guide them in their resolution of the conflict.

This points out the moral imperative that the leaders in an experiential education program ought to spend considerable time formulating what the goals of the program really are. Once these goals have been clearly articulated, it is necessary that the programs or institutions formulate fair and just practices to guide them in allocating both access to and attainment of these goals by students.

Given that the goals of most experiential education programs are educational in nature, it is useful to formulate two different categories of educational goals that are helpful to the individual versus group benefit discussion. The distinction is made between educational activities as **means** and activities as **ends.**

For a given educational activity to function as a means implies that the activity itself is serving as a vehicle to another goal. The activity itself is not the primary concern of the educational endeavor. For instance, the Mankato State University High Ropes Course was designed to be used as a means to human growth and development. The whole point of the course is to provide a setting where groups can learn lessons of trust, group cohesiveness, conquering of fears, and increased willingness to take calculated risks. These lessons are primary. The course itself is secondary. Most groups will sign up to do the ropes course, clearly wanting to achieve these goals. Oftentimes a particular student will take a very long time to complete the course, due mainly to extreme fear. This means that the other students are forced to wait and, at times, forfeit even attempting the course due to approaching darkness or some other time limitation. Is this fair? In this scenario, the ropes course itself as an activity is secondary to the educational goals. It is arguable that everyone can attain most of these goals without everyone completing or even attempting the course. This is where the psychologically sophisticated instructor can utilize techniques mentioned earlier in this chapter. The student slowly dealing with her fear on the course is learning the lesson of courage and her belayers below her are learning the lessons of patience and compassion. Therefore, it is arguable that the educational goals the ropes course was designed to achieve have in fact been

Chapter Nine / Individual Versus Group Benefit

achieved. In this sense it is possible that everyone has learned a great deal by allowing the slow student to take her time. Therefore, it is possible that the standard of fairness has not been violated.

For an educational activity to be an end in itself means that the doing of the activity, or at least the attempting of the activity, is primary and that the activity provides its own end. Not all groups who sign up for the High Ropes Course are interested in attaining the goals of personal growth outlined above. Some groups simply want to have fun and want to have an adventure. With groups like these, the instructor faced with an extremely slow student might evaluate the fairness issue very differently. It is possible that since the actual attempting of the ropes course is the primary goal, that everyone in the group has an equal claim to have access to it. If there are ten students and they have five hours allotted on the course, it would seem reasonable that each participant be allowed one-half hour on the course and if the student cannot finish in that amount of time, that he or she be required to be lowered to the ground, thereby ensuring equal access by the other group members. In this scenario **access to the course** is the primary goal. To deny the others their claim to this access in favor of one student gaining all or most of the benefit could be highly unethical, given the goals of the group.

One move I have seen made over the years is what I call the "big switch." Take the group that is on the ropes course simply to have fun. Suppose also that one student is going beyond his or her allotted time on the course. Suddenly the instructor looks at the rest of the group and begins group process techniques involving the educational goals of personal growth. The instructor tries to get the students to understand the values of self-sacrifice and compassion for the slow one. This would be to pull the "big switch" move on the students. Suddenly, part way through the activity, the goals of the activity have been changed by the instructor **without the students' consent.** This is ethically troubling because the instructor has changed the rules of group and individual benefit while in the middle of the activity. A move such as this gives power to the instructor, a power not previously agreed to by the group members.

The distinction between activities as means and ends does not in any sense rule out what was said previously drawing from Rawl's theory of fairness. It is quite possible that either of the groups might choose to sacrifice group benefit for the benefit of the individual. That would be ethically right but the proviso should be kept in mind that some sort of compensation should be supplied to the rest of the group members who did the sacrificing.

Practitioners of experiential education should be acutely aware of the extreme complexity of the valuational conflicts inherent in any and all in-stances of group versus individual benefit. My contention is that this issue is one of the most basic ethical conflicts of the human situation in general, not just in education. One man needs a $25,000.00 heart transplant and 1,000 babies need infant formula costing $25,000.00. How should the $25,000.00 be spent? One man inherits a fortune which he will spend on private country club parties, while his neighbors are losing their farms to bank foreclosures.

I cite these examples in order to put the issue of individual versus group benefit into a much wider context of justice and fairness. The detailed situations vary greatly but many of the ethical conflicts are identical. The key point I want to end with is that judgments that are made by practitioners will be based on some standard of fairness and justice which mediates the competing claims of individuals and groups. The important thing is that those making the hard value judgments be: 1) conscious of what the ethical standards are from which they are drawing and 2) be prepared to offer rational arguments in support of these standards and judgments.

Endnotes / Chapter 9

1. John Rawls, <u>A Theory of Justice</u> (Cambridge: Harvard University Press, 1971), 60.

2. Rawls, <u>A Theory of Justice</u>, 112

Chapter Ten

Students' Rights

During a four-week wilderness course, a group of students were approaching day 12 resupply time. The two instructors of the group were quite pleased with the course and the direction it had been taking. The students were working well together and they had resolved several interpersonal and group problems to the satisfaction of everyone. In particular, the group had enjoyed the purity of the wilderness experience and were highly appreciative of being away from any contact with other people. As resupply came closer, the instructors decided it would be best if they did not bring in the whole group to the resupply site, since this meant exposing them to the trucks and to the other students coming in for resupply. Therefore, the instructors decided to have the students make camp away from the resupply site. The instructors took two empty packs and headed down to the resupply site. On the walk down they discussed the possibility of not picking up the students' mail, which the instructors knew would have been delivered by the driver of the truck. They reasoned that not bringing the mail would help keep the wilderness experience pure for the students. The instructors picked up the food, left the mail with the driver of the truck for delivery at the end of the course, and returned to the students' camp. Upon the instructors' return, the students were delighted with the fresh food. However, several students asked about the mail. The instructors informed the group that the decision had been made to hold the mail until the completion of the course. Several students expressed gratitude to the instructors for keeping the wilderness experience pure. One student became angry and charged that the instructors had violated his rights by not bringing his mail to him. Furthermore, he wanted the instructors either to go back down to the resupply site and pick up his mail or to allow him to go down to the resupply site to pick up the mail himself. The instructors informed him that the decision had been made not to pick up mail for everyone and that since the group was not in complete agreement about the mail issue, that his mail would not be picked up.

A special experiential education program had been put together, the purpose of which was to get young people of diverse cultural backgrounds working together effectively and humanely. There were several fundamentalist Christian students in the group and there were also several inner city juvenile delinquents. As the course progressed, the Christian students became alarmed at the extremely foul language being used by the delinquent students. A group discussion followed and the delinquents let the Christian students know that no attempt would be made to alter the foul language. Furthermore, the juvenile delinquent students claimed that the Christian students were culturally illiterate and that the Christian students were learning valuable lessons by being exposed to the foul language. The course instructors listened to the discussion and realized that little headway was being made by the group on the issue. Therefore, the instructors decided that a compromise would be in order. They proposed to the group that everyone agree that the Christian students would try to not be as sensitive as they had been and the delinquent students would make an attempt at least to moderate their foul language while in the presence of the Christian students. The Christian students agreed to the compromise. The delinquent students told the instructors to go to hell and asserted that they had no intention of changing their speech patterns to make the other students happy. Furthermore, the delinquent students argued that they had a right to free speech and that was the end of the discussion.

The problem of students' rights is one of the most complex and conceptually confusing problems of ethics in experiential education. One reason for this confusion and complexity is because of the diverse meanings of the term **rights** within the scope of moral discourse. Both the young man who wanted his mail delivered to him and the young students who were claiming that their foul language should have been protected as a form of free speech were appealing to their rights. The young man wanted something provided **to** him and the juvenile delinquents wanted protection **from** having their speech interfered with. People claim to have a right to health care, housing, food, and many other material necessities. People claim that carrots have a right not to be eaten and that trees have a right not to be chopped down. Other people claim that they have a right to eat their carrots and to chop down their trees at will and claim protection from those who would interfere with this right. I was in an interview with a young teacher certification candidate recently and she claimed that young people have a right to feel good about themselves. Clearly these are all very different uses of the term "rights" and they are not all compatible with each other.

Chapter Ten / Students' Rights

Before going into any of the specific issues of students' rights in experiential education, it is useful to articulate a working definition of what a right is. Once this is done, it will be possible to try to unravel some of the salient problems of rights as they apply to experiential educators. Philosopher Robert Nozick has written extensively about rights theory and he offers some interesting insights into the nature of a right. According to Nozick:

We can locate the place of rights within the ethics of responsiveness to value, by noticing that (generally) a right is something for which one can demand or enforce compliance.

-and later-

On this view, my right that you behave a certain way toward me would be a function of how you ought to behave toward me and of how others (including me) ought to behave toward you. My rights are constituted by the treatment you ought to give me that others ought to demand or enforce of you- or at least it is not the case that they ought not demand it. [1]

According to Nozick, a right has a special place within ethics. He is arguing that a moral precept that carries with it a corollary demand that moral precept be accorded special protection, to the point of enforcement, is a moral right. If I have a right to "A" and if you interfere with my exercise of "A," then I can claim protection from your interference. Concomitantly, if you have a right to "A" and if I interfere with your exercise of your right, then you have a claim to protection from my interference.

Philosopher Tom Regan has also written extensively about rights theory and he offers a conception of what a right is, which sheds some light on Nozick's definition:

What are rights? How is the concept of a right to be analyzed? Various answers have been given, ranging from the view that rights are individual's entitlements to be treated in certain ways to the view that they are valid claims that an individual can make, or have made on his or her behalf, to have one's interests or welfare taken into account. What is common to these answers is that a right involves the idea of a justified constraint upon how others may act.....the possession of a right by one individual places a justified limit on how other individuals may treat the person possessing the right. [2]

If I have a right to life and if you try to murder me, then I am entitled to claim protection from you. You would thereby be constrained in your choosing to murder me. In a sense, my rights limit your actions as they affect me and my interests.

It is important to understand that not everything that might be counted as a moral good is accorded the status of a right in the sense in which Nozick and Regan describe a right. Just because something is good, ethically, it does not follow that it is therefore afforded the special protections of a right. Suppose you pass a beggar on the street and you give him some money. Many would praise you as behaving in a morally praiseworthy fashion. Few would argue, however, that you owed the beggar the money as a rights claim from him on your money.

There is a distinction in ethical theory between a **moral** right and a **legal** right. Legal rights are those rights that are recognized and protected by governmental bodies and the legal system. Moral rights, on the other hand, may or may not be recognized and protected by government or the legal system. The notion of a moral right is much broader than the notion of a legal right. As Tom Regan has put it:

*First, moral rights, if there are any, are **universal**, while legal rights need not be. Legal rights depend upon the law of this or that country, and what is a matter of legal right in one country may not be so in another. For example, in the United States, any citizen eighteen years old or older has the legal right to vote in federal elections; but not everyone in every nation has this same legal right. If, however, persons living in the United States have a moral right to, say, life, then **every** person in every nation has this same moral right, whether or not it is also recognized as a legal right.* [3]

Just because black people could be held as slaves in Alabama before the Civil War and, indeed, the right to hold slaves was protected by Alabama law, it does not follow necessarily that slaves therefore had no moral right not to be held as slaves. Moral rights are not dependent upon legal rights. A moral rights advocate would argue that slaves enjoyed the protection of rights long before the Civil War forced the Alabama laws to recognize the rights of black people not to be held as slaves. Legal rights can be altered, created, or obliterated by those who make or interpret the laws. Moral rights are not subject to the vicissitudes of those who control legal rights.

Not everyone within the tradition of legal rights would agree with my presentation here that legal rights are somehow different from moral rights. Legal rights theorists are split between those who advocate that legal rights are very similar to moral rights and those legal theorists who would agree with the distinction between legal and moral rights. **Natural law** legal theorists are of the opinion that the rights of human beings are **not** derived from law making bodies. Rather, according to natural rights proponents, human beings have their rights simply by virtue of their personhood. For a natural rights theorist, when a government makes laws in accord with natural rights, that government is simply recognizing what is already there. Governments do not **grant** people rights, rather they recognize preexistent rights held by the people.

The **legal positivists,** on the other hand, argue that natural rights are fictions and that the only source of rights is from the makers of the laws. According to this view, rights are **given** to people and have no reality apart from the body or bodies giving rights. The distinction between a legal naturalist and a legal positivist is articulated by philosopher Robert Nisbet in a discussion about the differences between the United States Constitution and the Soviet Constitution:

That is the special significance of the Ninth Amendment (of the U.S. Constitution): "The enumeration in the Constitution of certain rights, shall not be construed to deny or disparage others retained by the people." The genius of the Constitution lies, in sum, in its explicit acceptance of the propositions that rights are human- namely they inhere in the condition of humanness and are not gifts of the state- and that the essential purpose of a bill of rights is to restrain government from transgressing upon these human rights.

This is a far different approach to the problem of rights than was to be taken by the Soviet Constitution. In it, rights of individuals are granted by the Soviet state. There is no recognition whatever of rights anterior to the state. [4]

In this quote Nisbet is presenting the United States Constitution as being based upon natural rights and the Soviet Constitution as based upon positive rights. Whether or not Nisbet is correct in his analysis of the differences between the two conceptions of rights as they appear in the different constitutions is not important here. What is important is the distinction between a positive and a natural right in general. Natural rights theorists would claim the same sort of status for their natural rights as I outlined above about the status of a moral right. They would claim that natural rights **are** moral rights. The conceptual conflict between legal positivists and legal naturalists, while fascinating, is beyond the scope of this book to treat in any more detail. Suffice to say that not all legal theorists would agree with the distinction I made between moral and legal rights.

In the opening example of this chapter the student wanted his mail delivered to him and claimed that he had a right to receive his mail. The second example presented students who wanted their rights to free speech to be protected from interference by the fundamentalist students or by the instructors. The two examples illustrate an important distinction in rights theory that will be useful to practitioners. The first example of the mail is an instance of the student claiming a **positive** right and the second example of the speech issue is an instance of the students claiming a **negative** right. (Readers should not confuse my use of the term "positive" here with the discussion immediately above about legal positivism. What follows below in the distinction between positive and negative rights, is a different sense of the word "positive" within rights theory.)

A positive right is a claim to be provided with something. If I have a positive right to X, then I have a valid claim to be provided X. The student who wanted his mail delivered to him was assuming that he had a positive claim to access to his mail and that the agents of the program (the instructors) were obligated to aid him in exercising his right to access to his mail. Even though the instructors had what they thought were very good reasons for not providing the student with his mail, if the student had a positive right to his mail, then these good reasons would not be strong enough reasons to morally justify denying the student's request to have his mail delivered to him. Notice that a slight distinction was incorporated in the example. The student either wanted the instructors to deliver the mail to him or he wanted to be provided with the time needed for him to go pick it up himself. Whether or not the mail was delivered by the instructors or time was provided for the student to go get it himself, both alternatives, if adhered to by the instructors, would have represented the instructors recognizing the student's positive right to access to his mail.

A **negative** right is a claim to be protected from some sort of interference by others. If I have a negative right to X, then others are obligated not to interfere with my exercise of the right to X. Drawing from the example of the students who refused to refrain from the use of foul language, the delinquent students were claiming that they should be protected from having the fundamentalist students interfere with their free speech. Note the distinction between positive and negative rights in the speech example. The delinquent students were not claiming that the program had an obligation to provide them with the means to speak their obscenities freely. Were this to be the case, then suppose there was a student who claimed a positive right to speak obscenities freely. Suppose also that he did not know any curse words. If he had a positive right to curse, the program would be obligated to teach him the vocabulary needed to speak obscenely. The delinquent students were not arguing that the program had an obligation to help them speak obscenely, rather they were arguing that the program had an obligation to prevent others from interfering with their right to speak freely.

Another way to describe the distinction between positive and negative rights is to say that the emphasis in positive rights theory is on **providing** and the emphasis in negative rights theory is on **preventing**. In the quote above by Robert Nisbet in his distinction between the Soviet and the United States constitutions, an implication is that the citizens of the United States are primarily protected **from** interference by the government in the free exercise of rights by citizens. On the other hand, Soviet citizens are provided with rights **to** many things by their government. For instance Americans have no constitutionally protected legal right to health care. Soviet citizens, on the other hand, have a constitutionally protected legal right to health care. However, as Nisbet

Chapter Ten / Students' Rights

points out, Soviet citizens do not enjoy any constitutionally protected right from interference in their lives by the government. As long as the Soviet government positively provides its citizens with their governmentally granted rights, it is acting as it should. As long as the United States government refrains from interfering with citizen's rights, it is acting as it should. Generally speaking, positive rights provide many benefits but protect against few, if any, interferences; negative rights provide few benefits but provide many protections against interferences.

Whether or not people actually have any moral rights is a question that is hotly disputed by rights theorists and jurists. What is not disputed is the fact that people do have legal rights. Where these legal rights come from is open to dispute but the fact that they are there is not disputed by many people. **For the rest of this chapter I am going to assume that people have both legal and moral rights and that it makes sense to think of these rights in both the positive and negative senses of what a right is.** Furthermore, I argue that experiential education programs that want to be ethically responsible must pay attention to the problem of students' rights and in some way or other recognize the rights of students. In one of the landmark decisions of the United States Supreme Court, *Tinker versus Des Moines*, Mr. Justice Fortas wrote:

In our system, state-operated schools may not be enclaves of totalitarianism. School officials do not possess absolute authority over their students. Students in school as well as out of school are "persons" under our Constitution. They are possessed of fundamental rights which the state must respect, just as they themselves must respect their obligations to the state. In our system, students may not be regarded as closed-circuit recipients of only that which the state chooses to communicate.[5]

Although the *Tinker* decision, as a legal matter, only prevents state schools from not respecting the rights of students and is not concerned specifically with private schools per se, nevertheless I cite *Tinker* because of its recognition that students in state schools are rights possessors because of their personhood. Whether or not students in private educational settings ought to receive the same protections that students in public schools enjoy is a legal matter that is beyond the scope of this book. However, as a moral matter I will argue here that **all** students are rights possessors in the sense in which Justice Fortas used the term in the *Tinker* decision, simply by virtue of their common personhood. The student as person and, therefore, as one possessing moral rights is a much broader concept than the narrow problem of the legal scope of the applicability of this Supreme Court decision.

If students in experiential education programs have moral rights, then it remains to be seen what some of these rights might be and how these rights might result in policy making and program practices encountered by practitioners.

If experiential education programs are not to become "enclaves of totalitarianism," it might be useful to seek guidance on how to avoid this possibility. Once again I suggest looking to the formation of the United States government for guidance in this matter. If one were to look for that which prevents the United States from becoming totalitarian, one would look to the Constitution. This would lead into the Bill of Rights as a unique protector of citizens' rights. Similarly, I think a reasonable move for experiential education programs to make would be to see if they have anything similar to a Bill of Rights within their own programs. Specifically, it might be useful to establish and articulate a "Student's Bill of Rights" within particular programs. There is an important and useful precedent for arguing for a student's bill of rights within experiential education programs, drawing from efforts by the medical profession to develop a "Patient's Bill of Rights" within medical settings. In 1972 the Board of Trustees of the American Hospital Association affirmed and adopted a "Patient's Bill of Rights". The statement contains 12 provisions that make up a patient's rights while in a hospital or other medical setting. Briefly outlined, it is affirmed that patients have the following rights:

1. *The right to considerate and respectful care*
2. *The right to complete information*
3. *The right to informed consent*
4. *The right to refuse treatment*
5. *The right to privacy*
6. *The right to confidentiality*
7. *The right to access to services*
8. *The right to know who is caring for him*
9. *The right to know if he is being used for experimentation*
10. *The right to continuity of care*
11. *The right to examine his financial bill*
12. *The right to be told of all hospital rules and regulations.* [6]

It is interesting to note several things about this bill of rights. First, all but two rights (privacy and refusal of treatment) are presented in the form of a positive right. Second, all of the rights presented are rooted in aspects of morality that would particularly be of concern to a person within the medical care system. Third, no mention is made of these rights not being exhaustive. In other words, there is no proviso made for the patient having rights that are not specifically spelled out. Fourth, there is an implication within the original document that patient's rights are conferred by the institution upon patients. Ethicist Willard Gaylin has written a critique of the "Patient's Bill of Rights" on precisely this point:

By presenting its considerations as a "Patient's Bill of Rights", it creates the impression that the hospital is "granting" these rights to the patient. The hospital has no power to grant these rights. They are vested in the patient to begin with. If the rights have been violated, they have been violated by the hospital and its hirelings. The title a "Patient's Bill of Rights" therefore seems not only pretentious but deceptive. In effect, all that the document does is return to the patient, with an air of largess, some of the rights hospitals have previously stolen from him. [7]

I present Gaylin's hesitations about the "Patient's Bill of Rights" in order to indicate a warning about the move to develop a "Student's Bill of Rights" as a possible solution to the problem of students' rights in experiential education. The ideal Bill of Rights for any person would be formulated in such a way as to protect negative rights; provide positive rights; cover the broad spectrum of possible areas of moral concern that may need to be covered within specific situations and contexts; recognize that people enjoy rights that might not be specified in the document; and, finally, recognize that people have these rights by virtue of their personhood, and not by the granting of these rights by the producers of the document. Obviously, such a document would be utopian and, as a practical matter, nearly impossible to produce. However, there is some mileage to be gained from Gaylin's objections about patient's rights as a warning about some of the pitfalls that experiential educators might encounter. What follows below are some key issues that will need to be considered by programs that may elect to develop a Student's Bill of Rights. No attempt will be made to write such a bill. That would be beyond the scope of this book. It is enough to outline some broad conceptual parameters at this point.

That students on experiential education courses should have certain negative rights protected is obvious. Clearly, students should have the right not to be killed through instructor anger or displeasure about a student's behavior. The staff members and participants of the program must not be allowed to steal students' private property. Students should have the negative right not to be sexually abused while on courses. Note that all three of these rights are already protected by the criminal codes of the state and local governments in which programs operate. It seems like a duplication of effort to take the time to rearticulate the preexistent criminal codes. Therefore, I suggest that individuals developing students' rights documents by programs recognize the reality of the criminal codes, although these codes need not be written out. A better use of effort would be to articulate negative rights that students ought to enjoy that may not be covered within criminal codes.

I recall a situation a few years ago that illustrates this point. An instructor on a wilderness-based experiential education program wanted her students to experience an overnight bivouac with no survival gear other than the clothes on their backs. She told the students that they were going for a walk after supper. The instructor led the students far from their camp. Night closed in and the instructor informed the students that they would not be returning to camp that night and that they would have to make the best of the situation. One student reacted angrily to the instructor's announcement and declared that her rights had been violated by the instructor, since the instructor had not informed the students that they would be going for an overnight bivouac with no equipment, before the fact. This raises the broader ethical issue about whether students enjoy certain negative rights (in this case, not to be impelled into unpleasant situations with no prior consent) that instructors and other program personnel are bound to respect. There is no law that would have been violated in this case, that I am aware of, but it is at least possible that in this case students' moral rights were violated. The point is that negative rights not already covered by the law, may need to be protected.

A Student's Bill of Rights ideally would cover students' positive rights. I suspect that issues of positive rights of students will generally concern access to the benefits of participating in the program. For instance I can imagine a student claiming that he or she has a right to use the safest equipment that is available when he or she is undertaking a potentially hazardous activity. Students may have a claim to a right of equal access to participate in all activities paid for by the student. In the opening example of this chapter, one student claimed a positive right to have access to his mail.

This raises the much broader issue of the complexity of positive rights which are claimed by students by virtue of their having purchased a service. I have no positive right to own a word processor computer. However, if I buy a computer from company X, I then claim to have the right to have that computer delivered to me promptly. My right to have the computer delivered was the result of my having purchased the computer. If the computer is not delivered, then I would say that company X has violated my rights. Since most students in experiential education programs are in the programs by virtue of having paid for the program, it would behoove programs to pay close attention to what positive rights students may enjoy as the result of having purchased the educational service.

I need to say something about students' rights and the whole issue of informed consent. Take the example of the student who claimed a right to have his mail delivered to him during the resupply. As I outlined the scenario, the student had not consented to have his mail withheld from him by the program. Therefore, he claimed that his rights were violated. The same held true for the example involving the forced bivouac. Many issues of violations of students' rights will become moot if the students have agreed not to exercise certain rights (positive or negative) while they are on certain educational programs. Note that I did **not** say that the students gave up their rights, only that they agreed not to exercise them. This is a major distinction. To agree not to exercise a right is very different from giving up a right. Logically, if being a rights possessor is rooted in one's personhood, then as long as one is a person, one cannot possibly give up one's rights. (This does not mean that one cannot have one's rights taken away as the result of criminal activity.) To agree not to exercise a right means that I still have that right, but that I agree not to enjoy that right for a specified period of time. If students have rights, and if programs want students not to exercise certain rights while in a program, then programs must be very careful to obtain informed consent from the students **before** they are asked not to exercise their rights.

If experiential educators are to take students' rights seriously, then it seems vital that, absent any prior agreement not to exercise certain rights, the burden of proof for justification of violating rights lies squarely in the lap of the program. For a student to claim protection of his rights, assuming that students have rights, requires no justification on the part of the students. This does not mean that programs will not be able to find morally acceptable justifications for violating a student's rights. For example, let's say that students have the negative right to free speech and that students have not agreed to limitations on this right. During a rock climbing class an obnoxious student insists on shouting "Rock!" just for fun because he enjoys seeing his fellows duck unnecessarily. The instructor on the scene insists that the student desist from speaking this way. The student replies that he has a right to free speech and that the instructor cannot violate that right. It seems clear that the instructor would be justified in abridging the student's right to speak freely because the student's speech compromised the effectiveness of the safety system that had been worked out, and, therefore, compromised the safety of the other students. The instructor could well argue that that student did in fact give consent to abide by the safety procedures of the program and that his exercise of his free speech in this instance violated the safety procedures which the student had already agreed upon.

The example of the student shouting "Rock!" is a typical example of a major problem with students' rights and their formulation as a Bill of Rights. Very often rights come into conflict. In the above example the student's free speech right came into direct conflict with the other students' right to a safe program.

If the instructor who interfered with the student's free speech were required to justify his actions, he would probably use the argument that, because of the harm that would result from the student's speaking freely, he was justified in interfering with the student's free speech. The invoking of the harm principle to justify interferences with rights is common and a very compelling argument.

The harm principle, however, has dangers lurking within it. One might argue that harming means having a negative affect on others' interests. The fundamentalist students in the opening example of this chapter might argue that they were harmed ("negatively affected") by the other students' profanity and that, therefore, the instructors were morally obliged to interfere with the delinquent students' free speech, just as the instructors were obligated to interfere with the free speech rights of the student shouting "Rock!" unnecessarily. It is my view that simply having a negative effect on someone else's interests is not necessarily a sufficient condition for justifying interferences with the exercise of a right. Robert Nozick has a very interesting example of the point I am trying to make about the harm principle:

Suppose you own a station wagon or a bus and lend it to a group of people for a year while you are out of the country. During this year these people become quite dependent on your vehicle, integrating it into their lives. When at the end of the year you return, as you said you would, and ask for your bus back, these people say that your decision once more to use the bus yourself importantly affects their lives, and so they have a right to a say in determining what is to become of the bus. Surely this claim is without merit. The bus is yours... [8]

The point here is that you do not surrender your property right to your automobile simply because others are negatively affected by your decision to take back your car. My own view is that the harm principle is a good one to justify abridging someone's rights but that harm must be very carefully assessed. Simple psychological discomfort, as in the case of the fundamentalist students versus the delinquents, would not usually be a sufficient justification for interfering with the students' free speech rights. As a practical matter, when rights come into conflict, invoking the harm principle to resolve these conflicts needs to be done very carefully and with a clear notion of what, exactly, is meant by harm and how much harm or what kind of harm is enough to justify violating a student's rights.

Finally, if students have rights, then it will be necessary for experiential educators to take these rights seriously. The details of working out what students' rights are and how to resolve conflicts of rights will be a major undertaking. Indeed, even in the public school sector, students' rights are a source of a great deal of conflict. Therefore, it is reasonable for experiential educators to be prepared for a great deal of confusion and turmoil as they

Chapter Ten / Students' Rights

grapple with the problem of students' rights. In addition, many experiential education programs operate in environments and utilize certain techniques, like adventure-based programming, that will reveal issues of students' rights that other educators may never have encountered before. As the issue of students' rights is taken more seriously by practitioners, novel problems will emerge which should prove quite challenging to those making the tough decisions.

Endnotes / Chapter 10

1. Robert Nozick, Philosophical Investigations (Cambridge: Harvard University Press, 1981), 499.

2. Tom Regan, Matters of Life and Death: New Introductory Essays in Moral Philosophy (New York: Random House, 1980), 22,23.

3. Regan, 21.

4. Robert Nisbet, "Human Rights," in Prejudices: A Philosophical Dictionary (Cambridge: Harvard University Press, 1982), 167.

5. Tinker v. Des Moines Independent Community School District, 393 US 503 (1969).

6. Tom Regan, Contemporary Issues in Bioethics (Belmont: Wadsworth Press, 1978), 140, 141.

7. Willard Gaylin, "The Patient's Bill of Rights" in Contemporary Issues in Bioethics, ed. Tom Regan (Belmont: Wadsworth Press, 1978), 142.

8. Robert Nozick, Anarchy, State, and Utopia (New York: Basic Books, 1974), 269.

Chapter Eleven

Social Implications

The director of an adventure education program received a telephone call from an official of a large corporation. The caller wanted to schedule a team building day utilizing the high ropes course and initiative facilities. As the director and caller began to talk about the necessary scheduling details, the specifics about the corporation's problems emerged. The corporation had been assigned a contract with the Department of Defense to develop precision weapons technology for the Pentagon. The team which had been assigned the project was having a hard time adjusting to the new assignment and leadership conflicts had emerged. The official felt that an adventure education program similar to the one he had read about in a local newspaper might help get the precision weapons team on track. Hence, the call to the director. The director told the caller it would be necessary to contact the instructor pool before setting up the day's activities. He would call back after the instructors had been identified and assigned to the course.

The director then contacted several instructors to get the course set up. Several instructors were incredulous that the director had even considered setting up such a course. They felt strongly that the corporation they were dealing with was immoral and more specifically, they felt that this particular project team was not a group that the adventure education program should have anything to do with. One instructor stated that if the course was set up for the corporation, she would resign as an instructor.

A meeting was called and all of the instructors and the director met to discuss the situation. The group quickly divided, with one subgroup arguing that any interaction with this corporation would be immoral and with the other subgroup arguing it would be immoral not to work with the project team. Some felt that working with these clients would be a good opportunity for expanding

Chapter Eleven / Social Implications

the impact of the adventure program to a much wider audience. One instructor was excited about working with the group in order that he might change the workers' attitudes about working for the corporation. Another instructor felt that the corporation was doing a national service that was critical for maintaining world peace and that the instructors who objected to working with this group were themselves morally arrogant and misinformed about the importance of precision weapons for world peace. An impasse had been reached and the director had to make the final decision about the precision weapons team and the adventure education program.

Experiential educators do not do their work isolated and insulated from the world about them. Throughout this book I have focused attention on the ethical issues confronting experiential educators within the narrow contexts of their professional activities. It is useful to examine the ethical implications of experiential education in a much wider social context. Are there any ethical obligations that experiential educators have to the wider society? If so, what are they? If not, why not?

The opening example raises this issue clearly. As experiential educators interact with the world about them, the problem arises about dealings with groups or individuals who may not share the same moral commitments of those who run programs. What should experiential educators' response be to groups or individuals who may be considered immoral or antithetical to the educators' moral sensibilities?

There are several responses experiential educators could make. One way of responding would be to identify those groups or individuals deemed to be immoral and then, simply, refuse to deal professionally with them. Practitioners taking this option might reason that professional interaction with groups deemed immoral would corrupt the moral purity of the educators involved. This presents some interesting and ethically perplexing issues.

For one thing it is not at all empirically clear that interactions with immoral people result in moral contamination of those who are morally pure. It may be true that professional interaction with morally tainted people results in damage being done to practitioners but this is an assertion based upon empirical assumptions that are problematic at best.

The problem arises of just how immoral must a group of people or an individual be before he or they are over the line of acceptability. In other words, suppose members of Group X are deemed to be immoral due to their inclusion in Group X. However, it is the case that many of the members of Group X have many good qualities that make them as a group not totally immoral. Just how much weight should be given to these good qualities? Maybe no amount of corrective goodness is enough to override the overall immorality.

Chapter Eleven / Social Implications

I am always fascinated by individuals who refuse to deal with groups or other individuals because of the moral contamination argument. The assumption is that interaction with morally imperfect people may result in contamination of practitioners. If this is true, then the problem arises of whether those seeking moral purity are themselves morally pure. If they are not, then it seems absurd for them to do anything professionally at all, given the possibility of contaminating their clients or students. This standard presupposes a condition of moral perfection on the part of practitioners, which seems on its face to be absurd.

Another common reaction on the part of experiential education practitioners to groups or individuals of questionable moral status is to deny professional interaction with them, not because of personal risk to one's own purity. Instead the argument is made that helping certain groups or individuals will further an agenda, either personal or organizational, that is itself immoral. There is no doubt in my mind that the use of experiential education methodology to teach, say, concentration camp construction to Nazi concentration camp builders would result in quite well trained concentration camp builders. Practitioners might object to working with these people, not because of danger of personal moral compromise but because of furthering an agenda that is immoral.

That this interaction might result secondarily in personal moral compromise would be less important than the fact that the activities of the participants would be considered immoral per se. The moral onus, then, is placed upon the ends and methods of a potential student or organization rather than on simply keeping oneself morally pristine.

Absolute refusal to work with those whose activities or ideologies are completely unacceptable to practitioners is a logical option. I am reminded of Kurt Hahn, the founder of Outward Bound, and his refusal to stay in Nazi Germany. Hahn's final response to Nazism was to have no dealings with it either personally or professionally. Similar reasoning could be utilized by practitioners concerned with trafficking with immorality.

There is another option, however, open to practitioners. They could choose deliberately to work with morally repugnant clientele, not in order to further their agenda, but to thwart or change their agenda. Many experiential education programs are getting into the business of working therapeutically with disordered individuals. Take convicted child abusers. Experiential educators who work with these people do not do so in order that the child abusers become more adept at abusing children. On the contrary the whole point of the therapeutic relationship is to stop the child abuser from abusing children.

An argument can be made that it would be morally wrong not to engage in

Chapter Eleven / Social Implications

professional relationships that could result in people ceasing immoral behaviors like abusing children. Theoretically, one could argue that it was immoral for Kurt Hahn not to stay in Germany and resist Hitler to the bitter end. This was precisely the stance taken by one of the instructors in the opening scenario about the weapons team. One instructor felt that by working with this team, the possibility lay open for changing the attitudes of the weapons builders towards weapons building. To refuse to work with the weapons team would eliminate the possibility of changing or modifying the moral attitudes of the people involved.

This raises another consideration. Examples like Nazi concentration camp builders and child abusers are relatively easy ones to illustrate the move for experiential educators to serve as moral reformers. That murderers and child abusers are immoral and are, therefore, in need of moral change is hardly debatable. I suspect that most cases facing practitioners will not be this simple.

For example, it is not at all obvious or clear that anyone doing weapons development for the Pentagon is engaging in unethical behavior. Many strong arguments exist which morally justify the development of weapons. To argue for moral reform of people who may not in fact need moral reform is absurd. One problem is to determine which social groups need moral reform and which ones do not.

Another problem is determining whether or not attempting moral reform is feasible or realistic, given the realities of specific social contexts. Attempting to make a meaningful impact on a child abuser is more likely to be successful than attempting to thwart the drift of an entire nation towards Nazism. In this sense, both Kurt Hahn and those who use experiential education for the treatment of child abusers could be applauded for being both morally correct and practically realistic.

A key problem that practitioners face in this area is that of conflicting ideologies, both within programs and in the society at large. As programs define and identify who they will or will not interact with professionally, the most complex and divisive issues of political philosophy will arise. There is no escaping this. The same practitioners who object to working with defense contractors might well have no moral problem whatsoever working with groups who advocate eco-sabotage and violence against those who cut down trees or do other activities deemed to be ecologically unsound. Differing ideological commitments result in different moral standards for the use of violence to further social goals.

My assumption is that the same clashes of ideology operative in the larger social context will be present within the structures of most experiential education programs. Practitioners who are agreed on the efficacy of experiential education may differ drastically in their ideological commitments. The salient ethical issue here is how to resolve those differing commitments within professional communities.

It is tempting to eschew the possibility of resolving such issues and try to convert experiential education into an ideologically sterile practice which is only professionally concerned with educational technique. It can be argued that experiential education can develop into a marvelous educational technology that is value-free and leave issues of ideology to practitioners who use the techniques.

It is my view that it is impossible to separate ideological issues from so-called technical issues in experiential education. This is because the techniques of experiential education are always used by someone in some social context, and every social context has built within it some sort of ideological commitment or other. Two philosophers of education, Edward Stevens and George Wood, have discussed this issue extensively:

In every society, ideology functions in two ways. First, ideology is the dominant belief system that explains or justifies the status quo. For example, the notion of Divine Right of Kings was an ideology that justified whatever action a monarch might take.

Second, competing ideologies that challenge the status quo can usually be found in any social system. In opposition to Divine Right of Kings, for example, there arose in Europe the ideology of self-determination and self-government. It eventually replaced the ideology that had supported monarchical governments.[1]

Every experiential education context will have dominant ideologies and most will have competing or divergent ideologies. The point is that the attempt to sweep the problem of ideology under the rug and hope it will go away, while tempting at times, does not solve the problem at all. It only denies the problem.

Recognizing that ideological conflict exists, both within programs and between programs and the at-large social context, while necessary, does not suffice to solve the problem of deciding which groups to interact with professionally and which ones not to interact with. I am not so bold as to try to present a final answer to this age-old problem. One suggestion, however, that might be helpful is for programs to institute some sort of conscientious objector status for practitioners within the program. Conscientious objectors could refuse to deal with specific clientele who violate ideological or moral standards that individual practitioners hold. Instructors who simply cannot bring themselves to work with certain clients or students could be excused from these interactions with no fear of reprisal from program administrators. This model is used in teaching hospitals where physicians and other health care workers who do not choose to participate in elective abortions for moral reasons, can opt out. (It is interesting to note this move presupposes a commitment to an ideology of the supremacy of the individual conscience in moral matters...an ideological commitment which is itself open to controversy.)

The same could be done on a program level. Whole programs could define for themselves where the parameters of participation lie in moral and ideological matters. For example, I can imagine a program director getting a call from the Ku Klux Klan for an experiential education program and telling the caller that Program X just cannot work at all with the Klan, regardless of the Klan's motives for making the request. It could be a very revealing and ethically challenging task for experiential education programs to engage, internally, in a discussion of what the limits are for serving various social groups.

It is arguable that refusal to work with any group is unethical for experiential educators. I am reminded here of the medical and priestly professions. Recall that the man who shot Abraham Lincoln, John Wilkes Booth, was treated by a physician after Booth broke his leg. The physician's defense was that doctors are morally obligated to treat injured human beings regardless of what they might have done and regardless of the awfulness of the ideologies they might believe in. The same holds for most priestly callings, at least within the Christian tradition. Few ministers or priests would withhold spiritual succor to those who have done great evil or who believe in evil ideologies. It is certainly possible that all educators, not just experiential educators, are obligated by the practice they engage in to educate all people, with no distinction being made about the moral or ideological acceptability of students or clients.

One rejoinder to this argument would be to define the practice at hand and see if the practice precluded certain individuals and groups from participation in the practice. For example, I am aware of some physicians who refuse to accept patients who refuse to refrain from certain behaviors which will probably lead to ill health. It could be that these physicians are acting ethically within the definition of the practice of medicine in refusing to treat certain patients. Similarly, it may well be the case that the practice of experiential education must by definition exclude some groups or individuals which are antithetical to the practice.

Suppose that Program X had as one of its fundamental defining precepts the notion that compassion is a key value to be taught to students. Not to try to teach compassion to their students would be to violate the very reason for the program's existence. Suppose a group was to sign on for a program being offered by Program X and suppose, too, that the students had no intention whatsoever of learning about the value of compassion from the program. Instead, they wanted to learn other things from Program X—team building, for example. If teaching compassion is vital to the teaching of team building, then it would be impossible for the program to teach these students team building in the first place. Therefore, it would be reasonable to refuse to work with this group. Indeed, it could be argued that it would be unethical to agree to work with this group.

It is imperative for programs to become very clear about the goals for the programs. Goals help to define the parameters of the program and unless goals are clarified, the program itself is fuzzy about its mission. As a practical matter, once the goals of a program are articulated clearly, these goals can provide a guide for making decisions about the ethics of working with various social constituencies.

Each group being considered for inclusion in any experiential education program will have its own goals and reasons for wanting the services of experiential educators. The goals of potential groups and the goals of the experiential education program involved should be compared. The judgment could be made about the moral congruence of the two sets of goals. This judgment could serve to guide decision making about serving particular groups. Suppose Adolf Eichmann was to call and ask for a team building experiential education program for his top 12 concentration camp administrators. He indicates that what he wants out of their participation in the program is better, more efficient concentration camp construction. The experiential educator asks why Eichmann wants these camps. Eichmann replies that he is Hitler's main man for dealing with the "Jewish Problem." These camps will further the Fuhrer's dream. That is why Eichmann wants the team building experience to happen.

The experiential educator explains to Eichmann that the instilling of the virtues of compassion and justice are key goals of all of the team building programs offered. Unless Eichmann is willing to learn these lessons, the goals of Eichmann's team and the goals of the program are morally incongruent. Therefore, the experiential educator could decline to work with Adolf Eichmann on ethically solid grounds.

An alternative scenario is that Eichmann calls and tells the experiential educator that he is concerned with the use to which his camps are going to be put. He fears that they will be used, not for benign detention, but for extermination and he wants to equip his administrators with the moral courage to resist this possible use of the camps. Under this scenario the experiential educator might well decide to work with Eichmann, hoping that good might result.

A third alternative presents itself. Suppose the moral goals of the experiential education program and the moral goals of potential clientele are incon-

Chapter Eleven / Social Implications

gruent. I have heard experiential educators argue that the moral thing to do is to get the students in the course and then begin implementing the moral goals of the program. I have seen this happen with juvenile delinquent populations. It is argued by some that it is permissible to hide the real moral agenda of the program in order that the students come in the first place. The reasoning is that the great moral gain to be gotten by the students justifies being less than candid about the real agendas of the program.

This alternative is a classic model of the stark differences in moral reasoning used by consequentialists and deontologists. To use trickery in order to get students in courses in order to promote laudable social goals is a clear case of consequentialist thought at work. Most such consequentialists would couch the moral worth of the trickery in utilitarian terms. Look, it can be reasoned, think of the great good to be realized by tricking Adolf Eichmann into thinking that his administrators are going to be simply learning "team building" when in fact they will be learning about the importance of compassion and justice. Who knows, maybe we'll save millions of people from extermination. Wouldn't that justify tricking Eichmann?

No it would not, a deontologist would answer. The act of trickery would be to deny the very goals of the program itself and, therefore, the whole claim to moral legitimacy by the program would be open to question. To use immoral means to further a moral end would be conceptually incoherent from a deontological perspective. Readers can use the material in the "Deception" chapter of this book for further analysis of this example.

As I write this chapter, a worry comes to mind concerning the whole issue of social implications of experiential education. Practitioners could become bogged down in a sort of social fastidiousness that could result in absurd practices. I am reminded of the problem caused by imposing socially correct litmus tests for the appointment of federal judges. Many competent judicial candidates have been denied judgeships because they offend the ideological sensibilities of certain constituencies in the broader society. The same could happen to experiential educators. I think a genuine concern with the social implications of experiential education need not degenerate into a kind of witch hunt to root those who are considered morally impure.

Theoretically at least, programs could develop a method to determine whether or not potential students are morally correct enough to be admitted into a given program or school. If such a practice were to happen, the potential for offending students and therefore rendering the program ineffective would be very real. While programs that eschew any consideration of the wider social implications are ethically troubling, the possibility of experiential education becoming ethically arrogant is also troubling. Concern with social implications need not result in moral fanaticism and ideological pomposity.

Therefore, practitioners should never forget the social implications of their professional actions. On the other hand, I want to issue a strong warning that concern with social implications not be exercised hastily and with a blind eye to the complexity of the whole issue. This will inevitably result in a certain amount of tension for practitioners, but I suspect that it is a fundamentally healthy tension. Two pitfalls are always possible: social complacency and social fanaticism. Seeking the socially right path, while avoiding complacency or fanaticism, is what I am arguing for here. What this means in practical terms for practitioners can only be ascertained by those making these hard decisions.

Endnotes / Chapter 11

1. Edward Stevens, Jr. and George H. Wood, Justice, Ideology, and Education (New York: Random House, 1987), 149.

Chapter Twelve

Paternalism

Frank, a 26 year old insurance salesman, had signed up for a three-week-long, adventure-based experiential education program. He had come on the course for a break from the routine of his work and to experience the thrill of the activities offered. These activities included rock climbing, mountaineering, low and high ropes courses, camping and expeditioning. He was assigned to a group of nine other students and two instructors. Initially, he responded enthusiastically to the course and was an active and vital member of the group. Other members of the group were having a harder time with the course and three members, younger than Frank, were having a particularly rough time. Their problems lay chiefly in their interpersonal relationships and their emotional immaturity. As a result of the intense interpersonal conflicts that were becoming routine, Frank was becoming disillusioned with the course.

He discussed the situation with the instructors and attempts were made by them to help the group deal more effectively with the various problems they were experiencing. On day 10 of the course, Frank approached the instructors and told them that he was seriously considering the possibility of leaving the course. He had experienced most of the high adventure activities which he wanted to do and he figured that he had received his money's worth. He was becoming more and more exasperated with his fellow students' interpersonal problems. The instructors convinced Frank to wait at least one more day before leaving. That night a group meeting was held and it did not go well. Frank went to bed sure that he would leave the next day.

The next morning Frank told the instructors that he wanted to leave immediately. They began to try to convince Frank that he still had a lot to gain from the course and that he should consider staying. He responded by asserting that he did not want any more counter arguments and he just wanted to leave.

He asked the instructors to arrange for his departure immediately. The instructors said that Frank would have to meet with the course director before he could leave. Frank became very irritated and said that he did not want to meet with anyone else. The course director walked up and began to try to convince Frank to consider staying. At this point Frank became livid with rage and indignation at all this pre-departure counseling and persuasion and informed the instructors and the course director that they were treating him like a child and that he was walking out regardless of their wishes to the contrary.

Harold was a 33-year-old physician on an adventure education program. He was a member of the United States Army Reserves and had a thriving private medical practice. The instructors of Harold's group had scheduled a rock climbing and rappeling day. The rappel was to take place at the end of the day after all of the rock climbing was completed. The day went well. Harold enjoyed his accomplishments and proved to be one of the most adept climbers in the group.

At the end of the day, the rock climbing ropes were taken down and the rappel was set up. Several students went down the rappel and all agreed that it was a fitting ending to a fine day. It was Harold's turn. He looked at the instructor and mentioned that as an officer in the Army Reserve he had rappelled many times and that the safety techniques used by the Army were very different from the techniques used in the adventure program. The Army techniques were designed to allow for quite rapid descents, whereas the techniques used in the adventure education program were designed to disallow rapid descents. Harold asked the instructor if it would be permissible to use the Army techniques. After all, he reasoned, the Army techniques had worked well in the past for him and he enjoyed the fast descents much more than the slower ones. The instructor denied Harold's request. She replied that the Army techniques, while good training for combat situations, were not up to civilian safety standards and were not acceptable in the present circumstances. Harold became insistent and pushed harder for permission. He said that as a physician, an adult, and an Army officer that he did not appreciate the instructor's treating him as if he were incapable of making this decision for himself. Furthermore, he felt that he was being treated as a child by the instructor in her refusal to respect his request and told her that he deeply resented it.

These two examples represent the issue of paternalism in experiential education. Two medical ethicists have described paternalism in the manner in which I use it in this chapter:

Paternalism can be briefly defined as taking an action toward another person without his or her permission and justified by the action's serving the welfare, interests, and/or needs of that person. Since paternalism overrides the commonly-held moral principle of the self determination or autonomy of the individual, it can also be characterized negatively as interfering with a person's liberty of action on the basis of its serving the welfare, interests, or needs of that person. Although this interference is sometimes regarded as coercive, it need not always be viewed as forced upon others. [1]

Both Frank and Harold felt that they were being treated paternalistically by the staff members of their respective programs. Frank wanted to go home without the imposition of counseling and psychotherapeutic barriers to his leaving and Harold wanted to decide which safety system he would use on the rappel. In both cases, actions were taken that went against the expressed desires of the students. The staff members involved based their actions upon a genuine concern for the "welfare, interests, or needs" of the two students and the students did not agree with the staff members about what, in fact, constituted their best "welfare, interests, or needs." My concern here is the problem of determining what to do when disagreements arise in experiential education about what is in a student's best interests. Specifically, the problem becomes salient when the paternalistic move is made in response to these disagreements. When is paternalistic intervention in the lives of students justified in experiential education?

Harold Vanderpool and Gary Weiss, the authors of the quotation cited above, offer five logical criteria for the basis of paternalistic intervention in patients' lives by physicians. These five criteria can be very useful to experiential educators confronted with the same problem that physicians encounter with patients. Whether or not these criteria are morally acceptable must wait until they are presented. Vanderpool and Weiss write:

The logical assumptions of paternalism include, first, that paternalistic actions are usually taken toward others without their knowledge or permission, thus interfering with the extent of their choices as free persons. Second, paternalistic acts are justified as intended for the good or benefit of others... Third, as a correlate of point two, paternalism assumes that the doctor is benevolent and and will perform only those interventions that are likely to benefit rather than harm patients... Fourth, paternalism assumes that the person who takes actions toward others without their consent feels qualified to act on their behalf... Fifth, the paternalist acts benevolently in another's behalf by obtaining as accurate an assessment of outcomes or consequences as possible. [2]

How do the cases of Frank and Harold line up against the criteria presented by Vanderpool and Weiss? The first criterion clearly was met. Neither student gave his permission for the actions that were taken (required counseling, required rappel techniques). The second criterion was met (both actions were done for the benefit of the two students). The third criterion was met (the staff acted benevolently and with the goal of avoiding harming the students). The fourth criterion was met (all staff members involved in both cases felt that they were qualified to make the decisions they made). Presumably the staff predicted good outcomes (for Frank, that he would not leave prematurely and for Harold, that he would not get hurt through unsafe rappel techniques), which meets the fifth criterion. Therefore, both cases meet the five criteria presented by Vanderpool and Weiss.

The question that remains for experiential educators to face is whether or not these criteria constitute morally acceptable reasons for acting paternalistically towards students. What reasons could be mustered to argue against paternalistic interventions in students' lives?

One of the most famous and influential general arguments against paternalism comes from John Stuart Mill. In his book, On Liberty, Mill argues:

That the only purpose for which power can be exercised over any member of a civilized community, against his will, is to prevent harm to others. His own good, either physical or moral, is not a sufficient warrant. He cannot rightfully be compelled to do or forbear because it will be better for him to do so, because it will make him happier, because, in the opinions of others, to do so would be wise, or even right. These are good reasons for remonstrating with him, or reasoning with him, or persuading him, or entreating him, but not for compelling him, or visiting him with any evil in case he do otherwise.

-and later-

In the part which merely concerns himself, his independence is, of right, absolute. Over himself, over his own body and mind, the individual is sovereign. [3]

At first glance, Mill seems to be suggesting that any paternalistic interference with experiential education students' wishes and desires would violate the sacred inviolability of one's liberty and freedom, unless the reason for the interference was to protect other students from harm.

It would be difficult to find two more incompatible and diametrically opposed moral positions on the issue of paternalism than the positions presented by Vanderpool and Weiss in contrast to John Stuart Mill. On the one hand, paternalism is justified rather easily by the medical writers. On the other hand, a rigid barrier is erected by Mill between liberty and paternalism. For Vanderpool and Weiss, paternalism is justified rather easily when it results in good things for the individual. For Mill, achieving good things for an individual does not justify paternalism.

As a practical matter, experiential educators must decide what should be done in specific contexts with students. Simply understanding the theoretical differences between paternalistic justification and prohibitions against paternalism does not solve the practical problem:

One way to proceed is to frame the moral issue specifically within the context of the practice of experiential education. This framing can offer a helpful perspective on the moral issue of paternalism. [4]

One reason that paternalism evokes such strong reactions from people is that paternalistic interventions limit people's choices and liberty (Mill's point). However, whenever people enter into relationships with professional practitioners they voluntarily accept limits on their liberty. In a sense, whenever I enter into a professional relationship with a practitioner I do so because in my liberty, I am unable or unwilling to do certain things for myself. I am paying that professional to do certain things and to make certain decisions for me. For instance, I decide to go to the dentist for treatment. I do so because I cannot examine my own mouth very well, and even if I could, I lack the necessary training to make the examination worthwhile. When my dentist decides to use a certain procedure on my mouth, he does not ask my permission. I sacrifice some of my liberty when I sit in the dentist's chair. Indeed, I am willing to pay for the privilege of giving up some decision-making liberty by the act of consulting the dentist. Imagine one's reaction if a dentist were to ask the patient's permission for every act he did. "Do you mind if I use anesthesia X over anesthesia Y?" "Do you mind if I use drill speed A over drill speed B?" "Do I have your permission to touch this tooth?" If paternalism were not permitted to some degree in the practice of dentistry, then the practice would reduce to an absurdity with the dentist being so afraid of behaving paternalistically that he would be unable to practice his trade. When I go to the dentist I am paying him to treat me paternalistically.

Suppose, however, that while I am sitting in the chair, the dentist begins to ask me about matters entirely outside of his professional competence. He asks me about my discipline techniques with my children. I point out that I do not hit my children. He then begins to lecture me on the importance of "spare the rod, spoil the child" and continues to do so without my permission. This sort of paternalistic intervention in my life is probably outside the bounds of the narrowly defined boundaries of acceptable paternalism in dentistry.

Although paternalistic interventions in people's lives are inherent in most professional practices, they are narrowly defined and delineated. They are also predicated upon voluntary participation in the practice by clients. The cases of Frank and Harold are illustrations of this in experiential education programs.

It is arguable that the insistence of imposing various barriers to Frank's desire to leave the course was outside of the professional competence of the practitioners involved. Presumably Frank was mentally stable, sober, an adult, etc. In short he was presented as an autonomous being. For an adult like Frank to be denied access to the means needed to leave a course, without first submitting to hours of counseling and psychotherapy, may well constitute an immoral violation of his liberty. Granted, the practitioners involved were well intended and only acting in Frank's best interests. However, if Frank's liberty claim was taken seriously, simply being well intended and acting in his best interests would not justify the paternalistic interventions by the practitioners.

Recall Vanderpool and Weiss' notion that "...paternalism assumes that the person who takes actions toward others without their consent feels qualified to act on their behalf." Does merely feeling qualified to intervene in a person's life justify that intervention? If my dentist uses suture size A to close a wound in my mouth, does he do so simply because he **feels** competent to make that decision or does he **know** that suture A is the one to use? To reduce professional judgments to feeling is very troublesome.

Let's suppose that professional paternalism is permissible when done in the context of a freely chosen professional relationship for which a person contracts. It is very problematic to reduce the competence claims of practitioners to the expression of feelings. Suppose Frank was to look at the instructors and tell them their interferences to his desire to leave the course were an immoral restriction on his liberty. Suppose they were to look at him and say they felt strongly that he would benefit a great deal by counseling with them and the course director and he ought to submit to this counseling. Frank retorts that they have no knowledge of his potential for benefiting from the counseling. They say their feelings constitute a valid knowledge claim. Frank replies that their subjective feelings on what is best for him are not a reliable foundation for their claims. On the contrary, he has equally strong feelings.

Given that professional paternalism is morally acceptable within the confines outlined above, it remains for the practitioner to truly know what is in the best interest of his student. A correlation can be made between high professional knowledge and a strong claim to make decisions for students, clients, or patients. Concomitantly, a negative correlation can be made between low professional knowledge claims and weak claims for paternalistic interventions, even within the confines of a professional practice.

Whenever experiential educators rest their claims merely on their subjective feelings, it can serve as a strong warning that they are on very weak ground as far as the ethics of intervention are concerned. It is my view that basing claims to know upon feeling is probably the weakest claim of knowledge that can be made. I am not suggesting that personal feelings have no place in professional decision making. Rather, I am very suspicious about the reliability of feelings to determine the acceptability of paternalistic interventions in the lives of students while in the practice of experiential education.

Another ethically weak aspect about Frank's case is the issue of voluntary participation in a practice. Presumably, if my dentist does something strongly enough to displease me, I can get up and walk out of the office. Suppose the dentist refuses to stop lecturing me on my discipline practices with my children. When subjected to enough of his paternalistic interventions, I can sever the professional relationship based on my decisions. Note that Frank was denied the possibility of leaving the course without first submitting to what could be considered unethical paternalistic interventions. Once a move is made to deny access to sever the professional relationship without first submitting to the interventions of the staff, then Frank is being held captive by the program. For a more detailed discussion concerning holding students captive, readers should refer to my chapter in this book devoted to that issue.

The case of Harold and the rappel is very different. In Harold's case, he was denied his request to use the rappel techniques he had learned in the Army. How would an ethically concerned experiential educator reply if he or she were confronted by Harold and he used the same arguments that Frank used?

Recall my principle of the correlation between high knowledge and a strong claim to paternalism within the context of a practice. Presumably the instructor on the scene was professionally competent and an expert on rappel systems and safety. For Harold to argue against the permissibility of that instructor to make her own decisions about safety would be to deny her role as a practitioner. It would be similar to a patient telling a dentist not to use suture size A to close a mouth wound, when the patient's only knowledge of sutures was through a first-aid course.

It was precisely because the instructor was an expert on rappel systems that Harold voluntarily entered into a professional relationship with her. For him to suddenly insist that she follow his wishes on the alternative rappel system is to ask her to renounce her role as a professional practitioner. In Harold's case, he mistakenly believed his cursory Army rappeling experience made him as knowledgeable on the subject as the instructor. Therefore, the instructor could counterargue with Harold that she was morally obligated to protect him from himself in this context.

If asked why she refused to use the Army method of rappeling, the instructor could give specific reasons why the Army system was not up to civilian safety standards. As I argued earlier, her weakest reply would be to simply say that she felt that the civilian standards were superior. I am in no way suggesting here that the instructor ought to be arrogant and insensitive to Harold in her replies to his requests. I am simply suggesting that she has a strong basis from which to act paternalistically towards Harold. Harold has voluntarily entered into a professional relationship with an experiential education practitioner. This means that the practitioner is obligated to behave paternalistically towards him where she is professionally competent.

This also means that experiential educators are called upon to be very careful in making accurate judgments about where their professional competence starts and where it ends. There sometimes are tendencies for practitioners to see their competence expanding into areas where they may not be competent.

I am reminded of the way in which wilderness solo activities are presented. When the issue of taking books on solo arises, I have seen practitioners refuse to allow adult students to take books on solo. The argument is made that solo is a time for meditation, removal from distractions, contemplation, etc., and that the presence of books will distract the student from these goals. Students sometimes reply that they are capable of using books in ways that will not interfere with solo's purpose. Some practitioners paternalistically intervene on students' desires and forbid books on solo.

Other issues also come up about conducting solo, such as the minimum amount of water that should be consumed each day to prevent dehydration, safety checks, hypothermia prevention, etc. Regardless of students' wishes instructors must insist that students take sufficient water to prevent dehydration and sufficient shelter to prevent hypothermia.

It is arguable that the issue of books on solo is out of the realm of the instructor's professional competence, whereas the issue of water and shelter is within the competence of practitioners. If this is true, and if the instructors confuse the competencies with the incompetencies, then the danger of immoral paternalism becomes a possibility.

This does not mean that students cannot give their permission to be paternalistically treated by practitioners when operating outside the boundaries of very specific competencies. For instance, suppose the student who wanted to take a book on solo was to discuss the situation with an instructor and the instructor presented reasons why it might be a good idea to forgo the book. Granted, the instructor might not have clear knowledge about the issue, but she might have some helpful suggestions for the student to consider. The instructor simply might have a hunch about the benefits to be gained from a bookless solo. The student might allow himself to submit to the instuctor's paternalistic suggestions out of deference to the instructor's subjective opinion.

Freely accepted paternalistic interventions in people's lives do not present a problem to John Stuart Mill and need not be precluded here. It is the refusal to admit the limits of one's professional competencies within a practice that presents a problem, especially when this refusal results in coercive paternalistic interventions.

Chapter Twelve / Paternalism

A derivative idea of freely accepted paternalistic interventions is the whole issue of informed consent, which has already been dealt with in this book. A commitment to the ideal of personal liberty can accommodate professional paternalism through an on-going commitment to informed consent. When a surgeon operates on me, she thereby makes many paternalistic decisions on my behalf, predicated upon my giving consent. In experiential education the same can hold true. As I argued in the Informed Consent Chapter, there could be a symmetry between the degree of consent that has been given and the degree of paternalism that is acceptable. In Harold's case, he probably signed a consent form to abide by the safety procedures of the program, making his instructor's paternalistic intervention acceptable. Frank, on the other hand, probably did not consent to required counseling before he would be allowed to go home. If this were the case, then the paternalistic interventions would probably not be ethically acceptable.

Cults represent an extreme form of paternalism and there is a "cult-like" potential in experiential education that calls for attention. The attraction of cults to a wide variety of people has gained a great deal of attention in the past 20 years or so. The tendency of people to surrender personal responsibility for their lives while submitting to the dictates of a cultish social movement, religion, personality, or other self-destroying entity is well known. One key characteristic of cultish activities and entities is the extreme paternalism exhibited towards members and participants. People are convinced that they are incapable of making even the most basic decisions for themselves. As a result, personal liberty is replaced by paternalistic control over the person.

Over the years, I have seen cases where well intended experiential education programs bordered on cult-like activities. A chief characteristic of these cases has been the increased encroachment of paternalistic interventions in students' lives while under the direction of the program. All cults are paternalistic. Logically, it does not follow that a program that performs paternalistic things is a cult. However, there is a strong correlation between paternalistic methods and cult-like institutions. This is not the place to go into this issue in any more detail other than to issue a warning to professionals in experiential education of the danger of ethically legitimate, paternalistic interventions transforming into ethically unacceptable, cultish interventions in students' ability to make their own decisions.

Endnotes / Chapter 12

1. Harold Y. Vanderpool and Gary B. Weiss, "Patient Truthfulness: A Test of Models of the Physician-Patient Relationship" in The Journal of Medicine and Philosophy 9 (1984), 355.

2. Vanderpool and Weiss, 355, 356.

3. John Stuart Mill, On Liberty. Quoted from The Enduring Questions: Main Problems of Philosophy, ed. Melvin Rader. (New York: Holt, Reinhart and Winston, 1980), 559, 560.

4. For a detailed discussion of the technical sense of the concept of a "practice," readers should see Alasdair MacIntyre, After Virtue 2nd ed. (South Bend, IN: University of Notre Dame Press, 1984), Chapter 14.